THE
MODERN KNIGHTS
CODE

THE
MODERN KNIGHTS
CODE

Volume 1

Lessons for Knights in Training

Timeless Wisdom for Young Men
on the Path to Manhood

Michael Stonecastle

Published by Pathmaker Publishing

Copyright © 2025 by Michael Stonecastle

All rights reserved. No part of this publication may be reproduced, stored in a retrieval system, or transmitted in any form or by any means—electronic, mechanical, photocopying, recording, or otherwise—without the prior written permission of the publisher, except in the case of brief quotations used for review, educational purposes, or critical commentary.

This is a work of non-fiction, written to offer encouragement, mentorship, and practical guidance to young men. The views expressed reflect the author's personal insights and experiences, and are intended for informational and inspirational purposes only. This book is not intended as a substitute for professional advice.

Note to Parents and Mentors:
This book is designed as a foundational guide to support young men at the beginning of their journey into manhood—cultivating character, purpose, and personal growth. It may be used as a conversation tool, a teaching guide, or a prompt for deeper discussions about manhood, values, and responsibility. Mentors are encouraged to read alongside the young men in their care.

First Edition – 2025
ISBN (Paperback): 978-1-7345271-3-1

Printed and published in the United States

For Modern Knights Code-specific inquiries, please contact:
modernknightscode@gmail.com

For permissions, inquiries, or bulk orders, please contact:
Pathmaker Publishing
pathmaker@akopublishing.com

Cover design and interior artwork by Studio Pedroza
Interior layout and formatting by Studio Pedroza

For additional resources, mentorship content, and updates, visit:
ModernKnightsCode.com

DEDICATION

To the men of the Modern Knights Code community—you're the reason this book exists, and also the reason I haven't slept properly in months. Worth it.

To my parents, who would be horrified to find their names only in the acknowledgements, and if I didn't put them on this page, I'd never hear the end of it.

To the rest of my family, who haven't actually done anything for this book—but because I know how family politics work, I'm making sure no one feels left out. You're welcome.

And to you, the reader, who probably picked this up—maybe by accident, maybe out of curiosity, or thinking it was something else entirely. Stay a while. It gets good.

CONTENTS

Introduction.. *xv*

PART I: IDENTITY & INNER FOUNDATION
1: Who You Are vs. Who They Say You Are 3
2: The Power of Knowing Your Name 5
3: Embrace Your Flaws, But Don't Let Them Define You 7
4: Lead Your Feelings, Don't Follow Them 9
5: Being Alone vs. Being Lonely 11
6: Your Mind Is a Garden, Tend It Daily 13
7: Comparison Is a Thief, Not a Teacher 15
8: Boys Seek Attention. Men Build Character. 17
9: How to Become the Man You Look Up To 19
10: The Importance of Self-Respect 21
11: Stand in Your Truth 23
12: The Power of Your Choices 25
13: Personal Responsibility... 27
14: The Journey Is the Goal 29

PART II: HABITS, DISCIPLINE & SELF-MASTERY
1: Small Habits Build Great Men 35
2: Practice Over Perfection... 37
3: The 1% Rule: A Little Better, Every Day 39
4: Why Discipline Is a Form of Self-Respect 41
5: Self-Discipline Isn't Punishment—It's Power 43
6: Real Strength Is Forged by Challenge 45
7: Choose Your Struggle 47
8: Build Systems, Not Just Motivation 49
9: Morning Routines & Winning the Day 51
10: Evening Discipline: How You End the Day Matters............. 53
11: Clean Room. Clear Mind. Strong Focus. 55
12: The Discipline of Focus (Even When You Want to Escape)...... 57

13: Guard Your Gates (Eyes, Ears, and Heart)........................ 59
14: Nobody Becomes a Warrior by Accident 61

PART III: INTEGRITY, TRUTH & VALUES
1: Your Word Is a Sword. Don't Swing It Lightly.................... 67
2: What It Means to Tell the Truth.................................. 69
3: Even When No One Is Watching 71
4: Stand for Something or Fall for Everything 73
5: Strong Enough to Bend, Brave Enough to Stand 75
6: The Company You Keep Shapes Your Character 77
7: Don't Lie to Yourself—That's Where It All Starts................ 79
8: Speak the Truth—But Don't Use It as a Weapon................. 81
9: Values Aren't Just Words—They're Lived Every Day 83
10: Honour Is Earned, Not Claimed 85
11: Integrity Doesn't Shout—It Shows............................... 87
12: Your Reputation Follows Your Choices 89
13: Live What You Believe, Even When It's Hard to Do............. 91
14: Your Conscience Is Your Compass 93

PART IV: BROTHERHOOD & ROLE MODELS
1: Choose Friends Who Sharpen You 99
2: The Brotherhood Test: Are They for You or Themselves? 101
3: Learn from Those Who've Walked Ahead 103
4: You'll Outgrow Some People–And That's Okay 105
5: You're Not Meant to Walk Your Path Alone 107
6: Help Others Without Expecting Anything Back 109
7: Role Models Aren't Perfect, But They're Real.................... 111
8: The Strength in Vulnerability..................................... 113
9: Stand by Your Brothers, Even When It's Hard to Do............ 115
10: Build a Brotherhood Based on Growth, Not Just Fun 117
11: Find Your Tribe—And Keep It Tight 119
12: The Strength in Openness: Building Real Brotherhood 121
13: Don't Just Follow–Lead When It's Your Turn 123
14: True Brotherhood Doesn't Compete–It Elevates 125

PART V: HEARTS & HONOUR: LESSONS IN LOVE

1: Understanding Attraction—What Draws You In 131
2: Who You're Drawn to Reveals What You Value 133
3: Emotions Are Not Weaknesses—They're a Part of You 135
4: Setting Boundaries in Relationships............................. 137
5: Lead with Honour, Not Ego.. 139
6: Talking to Girls Starts with Confidence 141
7: Why Respect Is More Important Than Validation 143
8: You're Not Ready for a Relationship If You Can't Be Alone ... 145
9: The Right Relationship Will Challenge You..................... 147
10: Don't Lose Yourself to Please Someone Else 149
11: Earned Respect Matters More Than Easy Attention 151
12: Knowing When to Walk Away 153
13: Rejection Isn't the End of You...................................... 155
14: You Teach People How to Treat You 157

PART VI: COURAGE, CHALLENGE & PURPOSE

1: The World Won't Hand You Purpose—You Create It 163
2: Fear Isn't the Enemy. Avoidance Is................................ 165
3: Every Setback Is a Step If You Stand Back Up.................... 167
4: Run Toward the Fire—The Forge Is Never Comfortable 169
5: You Don't Need All the Answers—Ask Better Questions 171
6: Pain Is a Message—Listen, Learn, Then Push Through......... 173
7: Forge Yourself Through Challenge 175
8: Bravery Begins with Action 177
9: Courage Isn't Loud—It's Consistent 179
10: Don't Wait to Feel Ready 181
11: You're Stronger Than You Think.................................. 183
12: Step Into Your Calling... 185
13: Life Won't Be Easy. Choose It Anyway. 187
14: Every Knight Must Face His Dragons 189

PART VII: HOLDING YOUR GROUND WITH HONOUR

1: Being Strong Doesn't Mean Being Cold 195

2:	Masculinity Is Not the Problem—Lack of Guidance Is	197
3:	What Real Confidence Looks Like	199
4:	Don't Chase Girls. Build Yourself and Lead	201
5:	Your Body Is a Tool, Not a Trophy	203
6:	Find Your Voice in a World Full of Noise	205
7:	You Don't Have to Follow the Crowd	207
8:	Popular Isn't Always Right	209
9:	The World Will Try to Shape You—Don't Let It	211
10:	Be the Same Man Everywhere You Go	213
11:	Choose Character Over Recognition	215
12:	Honour Doesn't Follow the Crowd—But It Lasts	217
13:	The Power of Silence: Strength in Restraint	219
14:	Be the Example You Wish You'd Had	221

PART VIII: BECOMING THE MAN YOU'RE MEANT TO BE

1:	Start Becoming the Man You Would Look Up To	227
2:	What Kind of Man Do You Want to Be by 21?	229
3:	The Difference Between Impressing and Impacting	231
4:	Leave Every Space Better Than You Found It	233
5:	You're Just Getting Started	235
6:	Legacy Isn't Later—It's Now	237
7:	The World Needs the Gift Only You Can Bring	239
8:	Every Step You Take Is a Message to the Next Generation	241
9:	Be Proud of Who You See in the Mirror	243
10:	Write a Life Worth Reading	245
11:	Don't Just Live—Build a Life	247
12:	Lead Yourself Before You Lead Others	249
13:	Strength and Kindness Can Coexist	251
14:	You Become the Man You Choose to Be—Every Day	253

Conclusion *257*
Acknowledgements *259*
About the Author *261*

NOTE TO THE READER

This book isn't about perfection. It's about progress. These lessons are best taken one day at a time. Take your time with each one, reflect, and let it settle into your life.

Becoming a better man is a journey—and your journey doesn't have to be walked alone.

INTRODUCTION

I know how it feels to stand at the edge of the world and not know who you are yet. To look in the mirror and wonder if you're enough—or what 'enough' even means. To carry questions no one seems to be answering: What does it mean to be a man today? How do I build confidence when I feel lost? Is it wrong to want strength, purpose, and direction when the world keeps telling me to quiet down, sit still, and not be 'too much'?

If you've ever felt uncertain about yourself, your place in this world, or how to grow into the kind of man you'd be proud of becoming—then this book is for you.

I've been where you are. Confused. Frustrated. Hungry for meaning. Trying to figure out how to stand tall without pretending, how to be kind without being soft, how to feel deeply without drowning.

I know what it's like to feel the weight of expectations pressing in from all sides—while also carrying wounds you don't yet know how to name.

And I also know this: You're not alone.

You may not hear it often, but being a man in this world isn't easy, no matter what age you are. There are voices telling you to hold back who you are. To dull your edge. To apologise for your masculine nature. But I believe you were born for more.

You were made to grow into a man of honour, depth, strength, and heart. Not just for your own sake—but because the world needs men like that. Now more than ever.

This book isn't here to preach to you. It's not a list of rules, and it's not some impossible ideal to chase. It's a series of lessons—from me to you. Each one is written to help you build something that can't be taken from you: your character, your conviction, and your self-respect.

Now, I want to tell you something important. While you can rush through this book and finish it quickly, I encourage you to resist that temptation. These lessons are best digested one day at a time. Take the time to sit with each one, let it sink in, and truly reflect. The process of growth is not a sprint; it's a journey that takes time, patience, and consistency. If you follow each lesson at a steady pace, you'll find that what you learn will take root deeper than if you try to rush through it all.

My hope is that these pages feel like an older brother pulling up a chair beside you. Not someone who has it all figured out, but someone who has walked the road before you and wants to help you avoid the traps, climb the mountains, and keep your head and heart intact.

I may not be able to walk with you in person—but through these lessons, I will do my best to be here with you, every step of the way.

So take a breath. This journey isn't about perfection. It's about progress. And you're not walking it alone anymore.

With respect, brotherhood, and honour,

M

'The first battles you fight will be within.
Win those, and the world can't take you down.'
— *Michael Stonecastle*

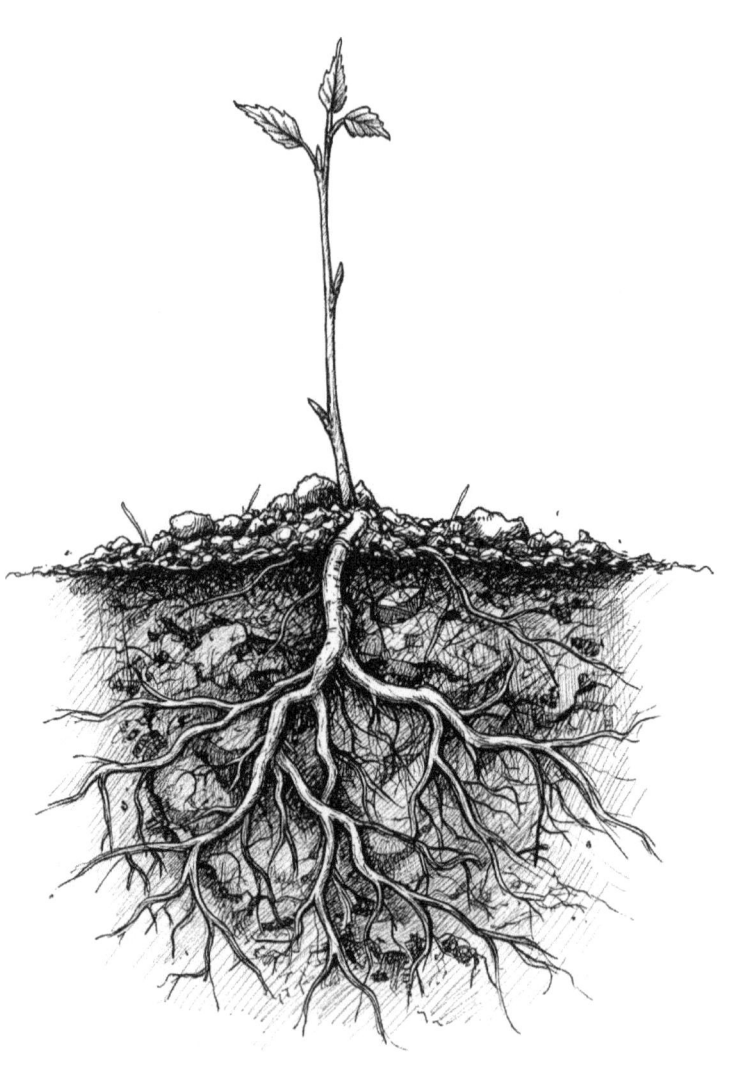

PART I
Identity & Inner Foundation

Every young man eventually faces the same truth—growing up is hard, and becoming a man takes effort. It doesn't happen by accident. This part is your foundation.

It's where you learn to stand on your own, face struggle head-on, and start seeing life through a wider lens. You don't need to have all the answers yet.

What matters is your willingness to begin—to show up, to learn, and to take the first steps with purpose and courage.

1

Who You Are vs. Who They Say You Are

◇◇◇◇◇

'The world will try to label you before you've even figured out who you are. Don't let them decide your identity. Discover your own voice and become the man you choose to be.'

◇◇◇◇◇

People are going to have opinions about you—and most of them will be wrong. Some will call you quiet when you're simply thinking. Others will say you're aggressive when you're just standing your ground. You might be labelled weird, soft, dumb, weak, too much, or not enough. And if you're not careful, you might start believing them.

The world throws labels like darts, hoping one of them sticks. It boxes people in and shrinks them down, often out of fear, ignorance, or plain laziness. But here's what matters most: you're not what they say—you're who you choose to become. No one else gets to define you. That's your job.

When you're young, it's easy to treat labels like facts. You're still finding your way, still figuring out who you are and where you fit. And in that confusion, you might start shaping yourself around what others expect instead of what you know deep down to be true. I've been there. It's exhausting, and it strips you of something more valuable than popularity—your voice.

You don't need to hold yourself back to fit into someone else's mould. You need to stand firm in your own shape. It's easy to be liked. It takes more to be respected. And real respect comes from being solid in who you are, not from pretending to be something you're not.

Confidence doesn't come from applause or attention. It comes from the quiet moments—when no one's watching, when there's no crowd to impress, and you still choose to back yourself. That's where real strength is forged.

So pay attention to what they call you. Pay even closer attention to what you start calling yourself. Are those words true to who you are, or are they borrowed from someone else's opinion? If they don't fit, discard them. Rewrite the label. Then carry yourself like it's already who you are.

Stand tall in your own skin. Be rooted in your own values. Because that's where real strength begins. And when you move through the world like that—solid, honest, unapologetic—the world can't help but take notice.

◇◇◇◇◇

▣ Reflection
Who has tried to define you in the past? Did you believe them—and why? Are you still carrying their words like they're true for you?

▤ Something to Write About
If no one else had ever told you who you were—what kind of man would you choose to be? Describe him.

✘ Challenge
Today, speak and move like the man you're becoming—not the boy they expect. Notice when you hold yourself back, and stand tall instead.

◉ Code to Remember:
I am the only person who defines who I am—I will never hand that power to anyone else.

2

The Power of Knowing Your Name

◇◇◇◇◇

'Your name isn't just what people call you—it's what you stand for. Every decision you make either adds honour to it... or takes it away.'

◇◇◇◇◇

There's something powerful about hearing your name spoken with respect. Not just called out by a teacher or mumbled during roll call. I mean really spoken. Like someone sees you—not just what you do, but who you are.

Your name isn't just a label. It's a signal. It carries your character, your choices, your story. The way you carry it teaches people how to treat you. It tells the world something before you even open your mouth.

So, let me ask you—do you walk like your name has weight?

Some boys never think about what their name represents. But men? They do. They understand that names are built, not given. That with time and effort, a name becomes something more—a reputation, a legacy. It becomes a reminder of how you've handled pressure, who you've chosen to be, and what you've stood for when it mattered most.

Every time you show up with integrity, you're adding value to it. Every time you choose what's right over what's easy, you're sharpening its edge. A strong name doesn't come from being perfect. It comes from being consistent. Every action you take—especially the ones done quietly, without applause—either strengthens or weakens what your name stands for.

You don't need a famous family. You don't need a perfect past. You just need consistency. Be honest. Be dependable. Be someone whose name gets spoken with quiet respect, not because you're loud, but because you're real. That kind of respect isn't handed out—it's earned.

And if anyone's ever called you something you didn't ask for—weak, dumb, bad, fake—you don't have to keep that. That's not your name unless you wear it. You get to decide what your name means, and you get to rewrite it if you need to. Every choice you make in your life will add to the meaning.

So walk like your name matters. Because it does. And long after you've left the room, your name keeps speaking for you. Make sure it says something worth listening to.

◇◇◇◇◇

💬 Reflection
If you could choose three words to describe the man you want to become, what would they be?

📓 Something to Write About
Write a list of labels or names others have used to describe you. Then write a second list: the man you choose to become, on your own terms.

✂ Challenge
For the next twenty-four hours, act like your name matters. No holding yourself back. No explaining. Just quiet strength.

⊘ Code to Remember
I will carry my name with pride, and live in a way that honours it.

3

Embrace Your Flaws, But Don't Let Them Define You

◇◇◇◇◇

'Your flaws are part of your story, not the whole of it. They're lessons, not limits.'

◇◇◇◇◇

In case you didn't know, I want to get something straight right now: everyone has flaws. Every man you admire. Every hero in history. Every person you know.

And yes—you too. That's not a weakness. That's being human. But here's an important thing to remember: Your flaws are not your identity.

Just because you've made mistakes... doesn't mean you *are* a mistake. Just because you've got weak points... doesn't mean you're weak overall.

Flaws are part of your story—but they don't have to be the title of your story. The key is to look at your imperfections with honesty and ownership—not shame. You don't need to hide them or pretend they don't exist.

Instead, use them. Learn from them. Grow through them. Let them shape your strength.

You can either run from what's broken or rebuild something better from the wreckage. And honestly, most people respect a man who's been through something and came out stronger—more than someone who pretends he's never struggled at all.

Some of the strongest men in history became who they were because they faced their flaws and refused to be ruled by them. They saw failure as feedback. They turned pain into power. That's what growth looks like.

So when you catch yourself thinking, 'I'm not good enough', stop and ask: Am I judging myself by my wounds, or by my will to grow?

Because one leads to shame. The other leads to strength.

You don't need to be flawless.
You just need to be willing.

◇◇◇◇◇

💬 Reflection
What's one flaw or weakness you've been hiding or feeling ashamed of lately?

📓 Something to Write About
How could you begin using that flaw as a source of growth or strength instead of hiding it?

✘ Challenge
Own one of your flaws today. Say it out loud. Learn from it. Talk about it if you can. But don't let it stop you from showing up as your best and most consistent self.

◉ Code to Remember
My flaws are real, but they don't rule me. I rise anyway.

4

Lead Your Feelings, Don't Follow Them

'Your emotions aren't enemies. They're messengers. You don't have to obey them—but you'd be foolish to ignore them completely.'

Some days you feel confident, sharp, and full of energy. Other days? Frustrated, sad, or just off. That's life, and it's going to happen. But here's a trap a lot of young guys fall into: thinking their emotions *define* them.

'I get angry too easily.'
'I must be weak if I feel this sad.'
'Maybe I'm just not built like other guys.'

Let's get this into your head, to set record straight:
You are not your emotions. But you can learn from them.

Think of emotions like signals. Anger might be pointing to something that feels unfair. Sadness might mean something important has been hurt or lost. Even joy tells you what matters to you.

But here's the important thing to remember: Emotions are simply signs—not directions, or orders you need to follow.

You don't have to act on every feeling. Just because something shows up doesn't mean it gets to take over. Real maturity is being able to pause, take a breath, and ask, Why am I feeling this and what's the smartest way to handle it?

That's called emotional strength. Not pushing feelings down. Not letting them control you, either. Just staying steady—no matter what shows up.

Feelings are part of being human, but they aren't qualified to drive your decisions. You are. That means even when you're angry, you can still choose patience. Even when you're afraid, you can still take action. That's how real men lead—not by ignoring emotion, but by mastering it.

When you learn to lead your feelings, you gain something powerful: self-command. You stop being reactive and start becoming intentional. You don't let storms inside dictate the way you move through the world. And over time, that makes all the difference.

💬 Reflection
What emotions do you usually avoid, suppress, or ignore? How do you react when those feelings show up—and what do those reactions teach you?

🎬 Something to Write About
Write about a recent moment where your emotions felt overwhelming. What were they trying to tell you—and what would it look like to respond with strength instead of being controlled by them?

✘ Challenge
The next time you feel anger, sadness, jealousy, or fear—pause. Don't react right away. Just notice it. Then choose your next move from a place of clarity, not chaos.

🧭 Code to Remember
I don't run from my emotions—but I don't let them run me either.

5

Being Alone vs. Being Lonely

◇◇◇◇◇

'Being alone isn't the same as being lonely. One can make you stronger. The other will try to make you feel weak. Learn the difference.'

◇◇◇◇◇

There's a big difference between being alone and being lonely. And I know it's something a lot of young men wrestle with—especially when you're still figuring yourself out. You look around and see other people always surrounded by friends, partners, or constant noise, and it's easy to wonder if something's missing in your own life.

But what you should know is this: Being alone isn't a problem. It's an opportunity.

Alone doesn't mean something's wrong. It doesn't mean you've failed or that you're behind. In fact, some of your most important growth will happen when it's just you, in the quiet, with no distractions. That's where you learn who you really are—without pressure, without pretending, without anyone else's opinions pulling at you.

Solitude gives you space to think clearly. It's a chance to reflect, practise a skill, read, move your body, or simply sit still and breathe. You get to be your own source of calm—your own foundation. That's a strength most people never build.

Loneliness, on the other hand, is different. It's not just about being physically alone—it's about feeling disconnected. You can feel lonely in a crowded room. And you can feel perfectly content, peaceful, and whole by yourself.

Loneliness isn't always solved by more people. Sometimes, it's solved by deeper connection—with yourself. So here's the real question: What do you do with your time alone?

Do you drift through it, chasing distractions, wishing things were different? Or do you use it to get stronger—mentally, emotionally, physically?

Ask yourself: What can I do to build myself right now? How you spend time alone shapes the man you become. Own it. Use it. The more you value your own presence, the less you'll settle for people or places that don't.

Let solitude forge you into someone who stands strong—whether the room is full or silent.

◇◇◇◇◇

▪ Reflection
When was the last time you felt lonely? What did you do with that feeling?

▪ Something to Write About
What's one way you can make your alone time more meaningful this week?

✗ Challenge
Spend thirty minutes alone—free from distractions. Use the time to think, read, write, or practise a skill. Notice how it feels.

❷ Code to Remember
I'm strong enough to stand alone—and wise enough to know when I shouldn't.

6

Your Mind Is a Garden, Tend It Daily

◇◇◇◇◇

'Your thoughts are seeds. Choose carefully what you plant, because your future grows from them.'

◇◇◇◇◇

Your mind is like a garden. Whatever you plant in it—grows. Each day, you're planting seeds: your thoughts, your habits, your beliefs. Some are helpful. Others... not so much. And just like any garden, if you don't take care of it, weeds show up.

Weeds of doubt.
Fear.
Comparison.
Distractions.
That voice that says, 'I'm not good enough.'

If you don't pull those weeds out, they'll spread. And they'll choke the good things you're trying to grow—confidence, focus, self-respect.

But here's the good part: you're the gardener of your mind. You're the one who decides what grows—and what gets ripped out before it can take over. You're in control of what stays and what goes. You can plant better thoughts. You can water them with effort. And you can protect them with strong boundaries—like what you allow yourself to focus on, who you spend time with, and what you tell yourself every day.

The work won't always be easy. Sometimes, the weeds will seem to take over. But remember this: you don't have to be perfect. Just keep showing up. Keep pulling the weeds, and keep planting new seeds. Each day is an opportunity to shape your mind into something better.

Don't just wait for peace or strength to show up. Make it happen.

Keep in mind, there's no rush. You don't have to do it all at once. Just check in with your garden each day, and ask yourself, what needs watering? What needs to go?

Because no matter what you may believe, your mind won't take care of itself. It constantly needs your effort, your awareness, and your dedication.

But if you tend to it daily—even in small ways—it'll grow into something strong. Something focused. Something powerful. And the more you care for it, the more you'll see your life change for the better.

◇◇◇◇◇

▨ Reflection
What kind of 'mental weeds' do you notice showing up in your thoughts? Where might they be coming from?

🎬 Something to Write About
Describe the type of garden you want your mind to become. What thoughts, values, or habits do you want to grow there?

✗ Challenge
Pick one positive 'seed' to plant today—a kind thought, a new habit, or a truth you want to believe. Write it down. Repeat it to yourself throughout the day.

⊘ Code to Remember
I plant thoughts that grow strength, not weeds that choke it.

7

Comparison Is a Thief, Not a Teacher

◇◇◇◇◇

'Spend too much time looking sideways, and you'll forget what's in front of you. Your life is yours to live. Don't waste it measuring someone else's.'

◇◇◇◇◇

Let's talk about something that can quietly drain your confidence: comparison. It's easy to fall into—especially when you're still figuring out who you are.

You see someone your age who seems to have it all together. Maybe it's the way he carries himself, his discipline, or the praise he gets from others. Instantly, you feel behind. You wonder, 'Why don't I look like that?' or 'Why am I not doing what he's doing?'

But here's something that bears repeating: comparison steals from you.

It doesn't teach you. It doesn't improve you. It just makes you feel small. It distracts you from your own progress and your unique path. Instead of focusing on what's ahead of you, it keeps pulling your attention to someone else's journey. And that distraction costs you time, energy, and clarity.

What you're noticing in others is just the surface. You don't see their failures, their doubts, or how long it took them to get where they are. You only see the result—and that leaves you stuck doubting your own growth.

But your journey is yours. It's not meant to be measured against anyone else's. Every person is at a different point in their development. Some may be ahead, others behind. It doesn't matter. What matters is where you are, and what you do with it.

You have your own race to run. Your own timing. Your own growth. And real confidence doesn't come from being better than someone else—it comes from becoming better than you were before.

So instead of measuring your worth by someone else's progress, measure it by your own. Are you better than yesterday? Are you moving forward?

That's what matters. Stay focused on your path, and don't let comparison rob you of your momentum.

◇◇◇◇◇

💬 Reflection
What are the situations or people that trigger comparison for you the most?

📓 Something to Write About
Write about a time you compared yourself to someone else. What did you feel? Now write what you didn't see behind their success.

✘ Challenge
Avoid the people, conversations, or situations that constantly leave you doubting yourself. Then, seek out someone you respect—someone who sharpens you.

⊘ Code to Remember
I will focus on my own progress—not comparing myself to others or where they are on their journey.

8

Boys Seek Attention. Men Build Character.

◇◇◇◇◇

'Attention fades, but character always stays. What you do when no one's watching is what makes you a man, not the likes or laughs you collect in the moment.'

◇◇◇◇◇

Let's be real—our world is obsessed with attention. It feels like the louder you are, the more you matter. It's tempting, and really easy to get caught up in it. You see other people getting noticed, talked about, and something inside you says, 'That's what I need. I want that too.'

Don't get me wrong, it's a rather nice feeling—but only momentarily. Here's something I want you to remember: boys chase attention, and men build character.

I get it. When you're younger, it feels like everything depends on how much attention you can get. Being the loudest in the room, making the best jokes, or dressing the way others expect. It feels good to be noticed. It feels like it's proof that you matter.

But here's the thing that most guys miss: Attention doesn't build anything of real value.

You can get attention for a minute, an hour, or even a week—but what happens when that attention fades? What happens when the applause dies down? What will remain is what you've built inside yourself.

But character? Character is something totally different.

Character is who you are when nobody's looking. It's the promises you keep. The way you treat others. The way you handle pressure. It's doing the right thing because it's right—not because someone's watching.

You don't need to be loud to be strong.
You don't need applause to be worthy.
Build a name that means something.
One quiet, honest choice at a time.

Because in the end, what will matter most is not how much attention you got, but the character you've built through your actions and decisions.

◇◇◇◇◇

▰ Reflection
Where in your life do you find yourself craving attention or validation? Are you acting to be seen—or to become someone worth being?

▰ Something to Write About
Write about a time you acted just to impress others.

What did it cost you? And what would you do differently now, knowing that real character is built in private?

✘ Challenge
Do one thing today that strengthens your character—quietly, without seeking recognition, and with no one else needing to know. Build in silence. Let the results speak later.

◯ Code to Remember
I'd rather be respected than liked—and I earn that respect by how I live.

9

How to Become the Man You Look Up To

◇◇◇◇

'The man you admire doesn't exist by accident. He was shaped, sharpened, and tested. And so will you be—if you choose to walk that path.'

◇◇◇◇

I want you to think about someone you look up to. Maybe it's a footballer, an older brother, a coach, a teacher, or even a character from a book or movie. Me, maybe? (Wishful thinking.)

Whoever it is, there's a reason he stands out to you. He's confident. Strong. Focused. Maybe he moves with purpose, speaks with calm, or handles pressure like it's nothing. He doesn't just seem capable—he seems grounded. Like he knows who he is, and he's not shaken easily.

So ask yourself this: What exactly do I admire about him?

It's probably not just the trophies, the talent, or the success. What leaves a mark is how he lives. The way he treats people. The way he doesn't complain when things are hard. The way he keeps showing up—disciplined, steady, consistent. That's what real strength looks like.

Now here's the part most guys miss: You can become that man. And you don't have to wait ten years, or hit a certain age, or have it all figured out.

Because he didn't just wake up one day and become him. He made choices—daily ones. Small decisions that no one saw. He trained his mind, his body, and his character when it would've been easier not to.

And that's what made him the man you admire. You can start doing the same. Right now.

You can speak with more honesty. You can train your body—even if it's just ten push-ups a day. You can learn to control your emotions instead of letting them control you. You can stand up for what's right, even when it's unpopular. You can start showing up for yourself.

Becoming the man you look up to starts in the quiet moments—especially when life pushes back. You don't need to be perfect to begin. You just need to decide that who you're becoming matters more than staying comfortable.

So stop waiting. Start today. Take one step. The man you look up to isn't out of reach. He's already within you—waiting to rise from the decisions you make right now.

◇◇◇◇◇

▣ Reflection
What are three specific qualities you admire in someone you look up to?

▤ Something to Write About
Think about a moment where you had the chance to act like the man you admire. What did you do—and what could you do differently next time?

✘ Challenge
Choose one quality you admire in someone and practise it today. Keep it small. Hold eye contact. Follow through. Do it even if no one sees.

◉ Code to Remember
I will act like the man I'm becoming—not the boy I used to be.

10

The Importance of Self-Respect

◇◇◇◇◇

'Self-respect isn't given. It's earned—when you do what's right even when no one sees it, and especially when no one claps for it.'

◇◇◇◇◇

Self-respect isn't about acting like you're better than others. It's about knowing your worth and treating yourself with the same respect you'd give someone you care about. It's that quiet voice inside that says, 'I matter. My time matters. My energy matters.' When you truly start believing that, it changes everything.

A boy might try to fit in, do what others expect, or act like someone he's not. He might think that getting attention or being liked is the most important thing. But a young man with self-respect? He stands tall—even when it's hard to do. He doesn't chase approval, hold himself back, or shrink himself to make others feel better. He knows who he is and what he believes, and he's okay standing alone if it means staying true to himself.

Self-respect shows up in every part of your life: how you talk to yourself, how you treat your body, how you use your time, and how you allow others to treat you. It's not just a way of thinking—it's how you live. It's about making choices that reflect your values, not letting other people or situations convince you to do things that go against who you are.

Here's the hard truth: no one will respect you more than you respect yourself. That's where it all begins. How you treat yourself teaches others how to treat you. If you let people disrespect you or waste your time, they will. But if you show that you value yourself, they'll follow your lead. And when they see you standing strong and true to who you are, they'll respect you for it.

Building self-respect isn't always easy. It means being honest with yourself, setting boundaries, and keeping your promises. It means dressing like you care about yourself, resting when you need it, and pushing yourself when it matters. Self-respect isn't just about thinking highly of yourself; it's about acting in ways that prove you value who you are.

Once you start living with self-respect, you'll never look back. And others will start respecting you more, too. When you show respect for yourself, people can't help but notice.

◇◇◇◇◇

💬 Reflection
Do you treat yourself with the same respect you expect from others? Why or why not?

📓 Something to Write About
What are three ways you can show yourself more respect in your daily life—through your words, actions, or habits?

✖ Challenge
Today, do one thing that reinforces your self-respect. That might mean setting a boundary, finishing something you started, or simply keeping a promise to yourself.

⊘ Code to Remember
I will keep my word to myself—because every time I follow through, I will prove to myself that I'm worth respecting.

11

Stand in Your Truth

⋄⋄⋄⋄⋄

'Standing in your truth won't always feel good. It'll cost you things. But the things it gives back—clarity, peace, strength—are worth far more.'

⋄⋄⋄⋄⋄

There will come a moment when hiding who you are feels easier than being real. You'll feel pressure—maybe from your friends, from social expectations, or even from your own doubts. Pressure to impress, to stay quiet, to blend in. And in that moment, you'll face a quiet but powerful choice: betray your truth, or stand in it.

Standing in your truth doesn't mean telling everyone everything or putting on a show for attention. It means being honest about who you are and what you believe, even when it's not easy. It's being yourself, even when the world around you is pushing you to be something else. It means not pretending to be fine when you're not.

Not laughing at jokes you don't believe in just to avoid tension. Not following the crowd when it goes against your values or causes you to lose your sense of self. It means checking in with yourself before checking how others might see you—because your own approval should matter most.

It might feel safer to hide behind a mask and blend in. But here's something to burn into your brain: being real takes guts. And yes, some people might not like it. They might try to push you down or reject you for standing up for what's right. But the right people—the ones who truly matter—will respect you more for standing firm in who you are. Over time, your honesty will attract better friendships, stronger connections, and a deeper sense of peace within yourself.

Your truth is your foundation. If you build your life on anything less, you'll start to feel lost, like something's missing. But when you stay rooted in who you are—quietly, confidently—you become unshakeable. You won't need to prove yourself to anyone. The strength to just be you will speak for itself.

You don't need to have it all figured out right now. Life doesn't work that way. But every time you speak or act from a place of truth, you take another step toward becoming a man of honour. And that's something no one can take from you. So, when the pressure to fit in comes, remember: standing in your truth is what will set you apart and make you stronger.

◇◇◇◇◇

💬 Reflection
When have you stayed silent to keep the peace, even though it didn't sit right with you?

📓 Something to Write About
What parts of yourself have you been hiding or holding back to fit in? What truth do you need to start standing in more?

⚔ Challenge
Speak up today. Even if it's small, say or do something that aligns with your truth—even if it feels awkward or risky.

◉ Code to Remember
I will not hold myself back just to be accepted. I will speak and live what's true.

12

The Power of Your Choices

◇◇◇◇◇

'Every choice you make is a step—either toward the man you want to be, or away from him.'

◇◇◇◇◇

Here's one very true thing that a lot of guys—both young and old—often overlook: You are where you are because of the choices you've made. Not fate. Not luck. Not other people. You.

Every single day, you make hundreds of decisions—many without even realising it. What time you wake up in the morning. What you choose to focus on. How you speak to others. Whether you keep your word or let it slip. Whether you follow through on your goals, or give up halfway.

These might seem like small things, but they actually shape your entire life. You are the result of your past choices. The man you will become depends on the ones you make next. That's real power. But it's also a heavy responsibility.

Don't just drift through your days, letting your emotions or other people make your decisions for you. Instead, pause. Think carefully. Ask yourself: Does this choice align with the man I'm trying to become?

Even when you don't see results immediately, your choices are quietly stacking up behind the scenes. Every bit of effort you put into your health, your mindset, and your relationships compounds over time—building the foundation for your future.

Want to get stronger? Train consistently.
Want to earn self-respect? Keep your promises, especially to yourself.
Want better friends? Surround yourself with people who lift you up.
Want a different future? Start new habits today.

This isn't about being perfect. You will mess up—we all do. What truly matters is whether you learn from those mistakes. Whether you keep choosing better, even after setbacks.

Blaming others may feel easier, but it keeps you powerless. Owning your choices—that's how you take control.

So own them. The tough ones. The small ones.
Because your choices shape your future far more than you realise.
And the better your choices, the better your life becomes.

◇◇◇◇◇

▰ Reflection
What's one recent decision you made that moved you closer to—or further from—who you want to be?

▰ Something to Write About
Think of a choice you often make—something small, but regular (daily or weekly). How could you make that decision more intentional, more aligned with who you're trying to become?

✕ Challenge
Catch yourself before you act on impulse. Pause. Ask yourself: Will this bring me closer to the man I want to become? Then make your choice with purpose.

◉ Code to Remember
I will take full ownership of my choices—win or lose, I'm responsible.

13

Personal Responsibility

◇◇◇◇◇

'A boy points fingers. A man takes ownership. You don't get stronger by blaming the world—you get stronger by building yourself.'

◇◇◇◇◇

One of the fastest ways to grow into the man you want to be is this: take full responsibility. For everything. Not just your wins, but your mistakes, too. Your reactions. Your attitude. Even how you handle things when life feels unfair.

It's easy to point fingers—to blame your parents, your school, the system, or your past. But blame is a trap. It makes you feel like you've got no power. And the longer you stay in that mindset, the longer you stay stuck. Responsibility is what moves you forward.

You might not control what happens to you. You won't always get to choose what life throws at you. But you always—and I mean always—get to choose how you respond. That's your power. That's your freedom. And that's what separates boys from men.

When you start owning your choices—even the ones that led to failure—you stop waiting for someone else to fix your life.

You stop making excuses. You stop needing someone to blame. You take back control. And that's when everything will start to shift.

The strongest men you'll ever meet aren't the ones who had it easy. They're the ones who say, 'This is on me. I own it. And I'm going to grow from it.'

They don't run from their story. They build from it.
They learn. They adjust. They keep showing up.

Responsibility doesn't mean perfection. It means being honest—with yourself first. It means checking your ego and facing the facts, even when they're hard to look at. It means choosing action over excuses. Growth over comfort.

When you take full ownership of your life, you stop being a passenger. You become the one steering the wheel.

No one's coming to write your future for you.
No one's going to hand you purpose, confidence, discipline, or direction. That's your job. That's your responsibility.

So grab the pen. And start writing a story you'll be proud of.

◇◇◇◇◇

💬 Reflection
Where in your life have you been blaming others instead of taking ownership?

📓 Something to Write About
Write about a mistake you've made recently. What would it look like to take full responsibility for it? What can you learn from it?

✘ Challenge
Today, catch yourself the moment you want to make an excuse. Pause. Take a breath. And own it instead.

⊘ Code to Remember
I will take responsibility for my life. I will not blame. I will not make excuses. I will own my growth.

14

The Journey Is the Goal

⋄⋄⋄⋄⋄

'You don't become a man at the finish line—you become one every step you take.'

⋄⋄⋄⋄⋄

Let me give you a piece of advice that will save you loads of headache in the long run: the real value of your life isn't found in reaching the destination, but in how you travel the road. You've probably heard that once you get the job, the body, the girl, the recognition—everything will fall into place, and you'll be happy then. But that mindset traps you.

Here's the thing I wish someone had told me when I was younger: whatever goal you set for yourself will never be the end. There's always a new goal. Another finish line. An even higher mountain to climb. And if you wait to feel satisfied only when you've reached that one elusive goal, you'll find yourself constantly chasing the next one, never feeling truly content.

The key is to learn to love the journey—the process, the growth, the lessons you pick up along the way. It's in the days when you don't feel like doing the work. It's in the failures you have to bounce back from. It's in the quiet moments of self-reflection when you realise you're becoming the man you've always wanted to be, even when no one's looking.

That's where the real change happens—when no one's watching, but you're still showing up. Every time you do that, you build something inside that can't be taken away. That effort, even when it feels unnoticed, is what separates boys from men.

Remember this: the most important part of any journey is how you travel. How you show up each day, even when things aren't perfect. That's where your character is forged. That's where you learn resilience, discipline, and patience.

Too many young men think they'll be happy when they reach their goal. But I'll tell you this: your happiness, your sense of fulfilment, your confidence, doesn't come from the goal. It comes from the journey itself. It comes from learning how to embrace the small victories along the way.

So as you walk your path, learn to appreciate the process. Celebrate the progress you've made, not just the finish line. Keep going, keep growing, and remember that your journey is just as valuable as the destination.

◇◇◇◇◇

💬 Reflection
What goal have you been chasing lately—so intensely, perhaps—that you've forgotten to stop and appreciate how far you've already come?

📓 Something to Write About
Describe a time when you grew stronger through the process, even if you didn't reach your goal. What did that teach you?

✘ Challenge
Do something today that reflects your growth—whether it's showing up with discipline, helping someone, or simply taking a deep breath and being present.

⊘ Code to Remember
I don't live for the finish line. I live to walk my path with purpose.

PART II

Habits, Discipline & Self-Mastery

Discipline is never about perfection—it's about consistency, especially when motivation fades and things get hard. The small habits you repeat every day will either shape the man you're becoming or slowly pull you off course.

This part is about taking ownership—of your mind, your body, and your choices. You'll learn how to build routines that serve you, stay focused under pressure, and keep moving forward even when it's uncomfortable.

Because real self-mastery doesn't come easy—but it's always worth it.

1

Small Habits Build Great Men

◇◇◇◇

'Greatness isn't a stroke of luck. It's built, piece by piece, every day. One small habit at a time. That's how men are made.'

◇◇◇◇

We often think greatness comes from big moments—winning a championship, landing the dream job, achieving some huge goal. Honestly speaking, greatness is built in the quiet, unnoticed moments. It's found in the small, daily habits that no one claps for.

The way you speak to yourself in the mirror.
The way you make your bed every morning without being told.
The way you show up even when it's hard for you to do.

These small things may not seem like much now, but they stack. Over time, they become the foundation of your strength, focus, and resilience. You don't become a disciplined man overnight. You become one by choosing discipline in the little things—consistently.

Every great man you admire started with small decisions: to get up early, to train when tired, to speak the truth, to learn instead of waste time. These choices build on each other like bricks. Bit by bit, day by day.

You might think no one notices the little things you do—but they matter. They shape your mindset. They prepare you for the bigger challenges life will throw your way. When a storm hits, it's not your dreams or goals that hold you steady—it's your habits. What you've trained yourself to do every single day.

Small habits are like seeds. You plant them through repetition, and they grow into character. Patience. Grit. Integrity. You don't rise to the level of your goals—you fall to the level of your systems. And your systems are built on habits.

Start small, but stay consistent.
Pick one habit and do it well. Then another. And another.

Because every time you choose to act with intention, you're building a man you can be proud of.

Greatness isn't a moment. It's a pattern. Build it, one choice at a time. And never underestimate the compound power of doing the right thing—especially when no one's watching.

◇◇◇◇◇

💬 Reflection
What small daily habit do you already have that builds strength, focus, or discipline in your life?

📓 Something to Write About
List three small habits you could start today that would improve your future. Pick one and commit to doing it for the next seven days.

✖ Challenge
Start with one habit. Keep it simple. Do it every day this week, and track your progress. Notice how it shifts your mindset.

🧭 Code To Remember:
My habits are my training ground. When I master them, I master myself.

2

Practice Over Perfection

◇◇◇◇◇

'Perfection is a lie. Practice is real. Progress is what counts. Focus on the grind, and the perfection will come.'

◇◇◇◇◇

Perfection is a lie. It sounds noble—something to aim for—but chasing perfection will drain you. It will make you second-guess yourself, delay action, and constantly feel like you're not good enough. And that mindset is a trap. It keeps you from doing the one thing that actually leads to growth: practice.

The strongest men you'll ever meet didn't get that way by being perfect. They got that way by showing up, again and again, even when they failed. Especially when they failed. Because failure teaches. Struggle sharpens. And repetition builds mastery.

You're not supposed to have it all figured out. You're supposed to try. To stumble. To learn. To get back up. That's how real progress is made. Perfection is rigid. Practice is flexible. And flexibility is what helps you adapt, grow, and keep moving forward.

When you aim for perfection, you hold yourself to a standard you can't meet. But when you commit to practice, every step becomes a win—even the messy ones. You turn mistakes into lessons. You build muscle, not just physically, but mentally and emotionally.

It's in the reps. The awkward conversations. The early mornings. The days when you feel like quitting but don't. Practice teaches you to push through resistance, to keep showing up when it's boring, and to keep aiming higher even when you fall short.

The goal isn't to be flawless. The goal is to get a little better each day. Small improvements, stacked over time, create powerful results.

So give yourself room to grow. Allow yourself to be a beginner. And remember this—every master you've ever seen or heard of was once a novice. The difference is, they kept practising when no one was watching.

Like I said earlier, perfection is a lie. Practice is the path you should follow. But make sure it's a path that leads somewhere. Make sure you keep showing up—especially on the hard days. Because that's how men are made.

◇◇◇◇◇

💬 Reflection
Where in your life are you avoiding something because you're not 'good enough' yet? What might change if you focused on consistent effort instead of perfect results?

📓 Something to Write About
Describe a time when practice led to real growth—even if you didn't do it perfectly. What did you learn from showing up anyway?

⚔ Challenge
Pick one thing you've been putting off. Take small, consistent action on it every day this week. No perfection—just progress.

⊘ Code to Remember
I will keep showing up—because progress is built on practice, not perfection.

3

The 1% Rule: A Little Better, Every Day

◇◇◇◇◇

'Stop waiting for dramatic changes. Focus on one percent improvements each day. Small, consistent efforts may seem insignificant, but they compound into extraordinary results.'

◇◇◇◇◇

We often overestimate what we can achieve in a single day, but we dramatically underestimate what we can accomplish in a year. The 1% Rule is simple yet powerful: if you improve by just 1% every day, those small gains stack up. They multiply. They compound.

The beauty of the 1% Rule is that it doesn't demand huge, overnight transformations. You don't need to flip your whole life around in one go. Whether it's reading a few more pages, running a little farther, speaking up when you'd usually stay quiet, or cutting one bad habit—you're building something. Just a 1% improvement every day can turn into a major shift over time.

That's how progress actually works. Quiet. Slow. Steady. But real. You don't need to conquer everything at once. You just need to take the next small step. Then do it again tomorrow. And again the next day. That's where growth happens.

This is where most people go wrong. They wait for motivation. They think they need to make big, dramatic changes all at once. But the secret isn't intensity—it's consistency. Showing up when you don't feel like it. Choosing discipline over comfort. Great men aren't built in a day. They're shaped by the quiet effort no one sees.

And here's the best part: the more you do it, the easier it gets. That 1% starts to feel natural. The habits get stronger. You build momentum.

So when you're tempted to quit because your progress feels slow, remind yourself—this is how strong men are forged. One choice at a time. One step at a time. One day at a time.

Those small efforts you make today may seem insignificant in the moment, but when stacked together, they create the difference between staying stagnant and becoming someone unstoppable.

Keep stacking your 1%. It adds up faster than you think.

◇◇◇◇◇

Reflection
Where in your life have small, repeated actions—good or bad—added up over time?

Something to Write About
Name one area where you'd like to improve. What's a small, consistent action (just 1%) you could take daily that would move you forward?

Challenge
Pick one 1% habit—something so small it seems almost too easy—and do it every day this week. Track your consistency and how it makes you feel by day seven.

Code to Remember
I will improve by 1% each day, knowing that small steps lead to great change.

4

Why Discipline Is a Form of Self-Respect

◇◇◇◇

'Discipline is not a restriction—it's a declaration of self-respect. When you choose discipline, and you keep your word to yourself, you choose to honour your future and the man you'll become.'

◇◇◇◇

There's a connection between how you treat yourself and how you see yourself. And one of the strongest ways to show yourself respect is through discipline.

Discipline isn't just about rules or restrictions. It's about commitment. It's about saying, I'm worth the effort. When you choose to get up early, to train, to finish your work, or to stay focused even when you're tempted to slack off, you're telling yourself that your time and goals matter. That you matter.

Think of it this way: would you respect a friend who constantly breaks promises? Probably not. So what happens when you break promises to yourself—like skipping that workout or ignoring your responsibilities? Your self-respect takes a hit.

The more often you follow through on your word, the more your confidence grows. Not because life gets easier, but because you become stronger. More rooted. More trustworthy in your own eyes.

Discipline builds inner strength. It teaches you to do what's right, even when it's uncomfortable. It keeps you moving forward when it would be easier to quit. You stop needing motivation all the time, because your habits take over. You show up—especially when it's tough to do. And that's where growth happens.

Every time you make a disciplined choice, you're proving to yourself that you can be counted on. That you're not just full of talk—you follow through. And that quiet, steady self-trust is what separates boys who drift from young men who lead.

Discipline is how boys become men—not by force, but by consistency. And every disciplined decision you make is a vote for the man you're becoming.

So start keeping the promises you make to yourself. Show up for your future. You'll thank yourself later.

◇◇◇◇◇

💬 Reflection
When was the last time you felt proud of yourself for following through on something difficult? What did that moment teach you about your own strength?

📓 Something to Write About
What's one area of your life where you've been avoiding discipline? Why do you think that is—and what would it mean to face it head-on?

✘ Challenge
Pick one small habit that reflects discipline—something that can be done daily (like making your bed, stretching, or finishing your homework). Commit to doing it for the next seven days, no matter what.

⊘ Code to Remember
Discipline isn't about control—it's about choosing who I become.

5

Self-Discipline Isn't Punishment—It's Power

◇◇◇◇

'Self-discipline isn't a cage—it's your freedom. The more control you have over yourself, the more you control your destiny.'

◇◇◇◇

Discipline gets a bad reputation. Some people see it as restriction, as if you're punishing yourself by saying 'no.' But true self-discipline isn't about punishment. It's about power. It's about deciding who's in control—your higher self, or your impulses.

Every time you delay a desire for something greater, you're not losing freedom. You're building it. Think of an athlete training for greatness. Is it punishment when he skips junk food or trains through discomfort? No. It's purpose. It's honour. It's mastery. He's not weaker for choosing discipline—he's stronger because of it. He knows what he's aiming for, and that aim gives meaning to the sacrifice.

Discipline doesn't make life smaller—it makes it sharper. It turns effort into achievement, and choices into confidence. When you train yourself to do the hard things when you don't feel like it, you're not just exercising willpower—you're reinforcing belief in yourself. You're proving that you're someone who follows through. You're building a foundation of trust with the man in the mirror.

There's a quiet respect you earn when you live with discipline—especially from yourself. It's not about being perfect. It's about being intentional. About showing up, again and again, even when no one's watching.

When you choose discipline, you choose yourself. You're telling the world, 'I'm not a slave to comfort. I'm building something bigger.' The thing that most people won't tell you is that discipline feels good. Not always in the moment, but in the quiet strength you carry afterward. In the pride of a promise kept. In the results no one can take from you.

Self-discipline is a muscle—and the more you train it, the stronger it gets. You don't need to be harsh with yourself. You need to be committed. Every decision you make is a vote for the man you're becoming. Make them count. Make them matter.

◇◇◇◇◇

▰ Reflection
Where in your life have you mistaken discipline for punishment? How might changing your mindset help you use discipline to build strength instead of resentment?

▰ Something to Write About
Write about a time when choosing discipline paid off for you. How did it feel in the moment, and how did you feel afterwards? What does that tell you about the kind of man you're becoming?

✘ Challenge
Pick one thing you've been avoiding—homework, exercise, a tough conversation—and do it today. Don't wait to feel ready. Just take action.

❷ Code to Remember
I will use discipline to build strength, not resentment.

6

Real Strength Is Forged by Challenge

◇◇◇◇◇

'You don't become stronger by taking the easy route. You do it by facing what you fear, one hard step at a time—and refusing to back down.'

◇◇◇◇◇

There's something powerful that happens when you choose discomfort over ease—on purpose. It doesn't have to be extreme. It just has to be deliberate. That's the heart of facing challenges: every day, do one thing that's difficult, uncomfortable, or inconvenient... and do it anyway.

Why? Because most people avoid challenges. But the men who grow—the men who rise—are the ones who lean into the hard things on purpose. It builds mental strength. It sharpens willpower. It teaches you that you are stronger than your excuses. That you can push through discomfort and come out tougher on the other side.

What counts as a challenge will look different each day. Maybe it's waking up early. Having a tough conversation. Finishing your workout when you want to quit. Choosing focus over distraction. Resisting the urge to complain or take the easy way out. The goal isn't perfection—it's consistency. And over time, those moments add up. They carve grit into your character and build the strength to push through any challenge.

There's a reason the path of least resistance never leads to greatness. Avoiding difficulty might feel good now, but it costs you later—in regret, in missed chances, and in opportunities that demand more than you're ready for. Facing these challenges head on prepares you for those moments. It hardens your mindset and toughens your spirit.

Start small if you need to. Cold showers. Cleaning your room when it's the last thing you want to do. Taking time for quiet focus. Choosing silence instead of reacting with anger. Each challenge you take on only adds to your discipline—a quiet declaration that you won't fold under pressure, no matter how tough it gets.

Every time you do, you prove to yourself that you're not controlled by comfort. You're becoming someone who can face pressure, fear, and challenge—and keep moving forward with purpose. That's how you earn your own respect. That's how men are built—through consistent action and deliberate choices.

◇◇◇◇◇

▰ Reflection
What's one challenge you faced recently that pushed you outside your comfort zone and left you feeling stronger or more capable? How did it change your perspective?

📓 Something to Write About
Make a list of the things you tend to avoid in your daily routine because they're uncomfortable. Pick one to face this week. What's one way you can make it more manageable and stick with it?

✘ Challenge
Start today: pick one challenge and do it—fully, without shortcuts. Then do the same tomorrow. Track your progress for seven days and reflect on what changes in how you think, act, or carry yourself.

⊘ Code to Remember
I won't wait for greatness to find me. I will earn it—by facing every challenge with strength and resolve.

7

Choose Your Struggle

◇◇◇◇◇

'Life will always give you struggles. Don't avoid them—choose the ones that build you, that make you stronger. The right struggle is what turns you into a man.'

◇◇◇◇◇

Life will never be struggle-free. But here's the thing: you do get to choose which kind of struggle you want. The pain of discipline or the pain of regret. The effort of growth or the cost of staying stuck.

Working out is hard, but so is being weak and out of shape. Studying is hard, but so is failing and living with missed opportunities. Speaking up takes courage, but so does carrying the weight of silence when you know you should have spoken your truth.

There is no easy path. Life is tough, and it will absolutely test you. But the struggle you choose will define your character. Will you choose the path that builds strength, or the one that leads to regret? Will you choose the discomfort of growing, or the quiet torment of staying the same?

Struggle isn't always loud. Sometimes it's a quiet resistance—a battle in your own mind. Getting out of bed when you'd rather sleep. Walking into the gym when you feel like staying home. Taking the high road when it's easier to lash out. Choosing focus when distraction feels easier. Choosing honesty when lying would get you off the hook.

These small choices add up. They shape who you are, and who you're becoming.

The worthy path is often uphill. It takes grit, patience, and consistency. But it also builds your resilience, your confidence, and your sense of purpose. The struggles you face today will prepare you for the storms ahead—the ones you can't predict, but will need to be ready for. You can't avoid all pain. But you can choose the pain that leads to strength.

Choose the struggle that makes you stronger. Choose the one that leaves you proud, not ashamed. Choose the path that builds you up, not the one that breaks you down.

And when it gets hard—good. That means it's working. Keep going.

⋄⋄⋄⋄⋄

💬 Reflection
What kind of struggle are you currently choosing—one that leads to growth, or one that keeps you stuck?

📓 Something to Write About
Every path comes with a struggle. Would you rather face the short-term pain of discipline or the long-term pain of regret? Write about a moment where you had to choose.

⚔ Challenge
This week, when you face something uncomfortable—waking up early, doing the hard thing, saying no—remind yourself: I'm choosing this struggle because I know where it leads. Then do it anyway.

⊘ Code to Remember
I will choose the struggle that shapes me, not the one that breaks me.

8

Build Systems, Not Just Motivation

◇◇◇◇◇

'Motivation fades. Systems don't. Build the systems that will make you unstoppable, even when you're running on empty.'

◇◇◇◇◇

Motivation is like a spark—it gets things started. But if you rely on motivation alone, you'll burn out fast. It's powerful in the short term, but it's fleeting. What you really need are systems—structures that carry you when your motivation fades and you don't feel like showing up. Motivation is temporary, but systems are reliable.

A system is anything that helps you follow through without overthinking. It's a checklist to guide your day, a routine that sets your rhythm, a reminder that nudges you forward. It could be a calendar, a designated space for focus, or even a set of habits you don't have to think about. Systems reduce friction. They remove unnecessary decisions, so your energy can go toward what really matters—execution, not hesitation.

Motivation will fail you at some point. You won't always feel fired up. But when your day is built around systems, you don't need to feel motivated—you just need to follow through. That's where the power is: not in bursts of energy, but in consistency. In small actions repeated daily, even when the drive isn't there. In showing up again and again, even on the days you feel off. Each time you do, you train yourself to rise above excuses and emotion.

Systems create structure. And structure creates freedom. When you know what to do, and when to do it, you waste less time deciding—and more time doing. You train your mind to operate on discipline, not emotion. You begin to rely on rhythm, not resistance.

Anyone can be disciplined on their best day, when everything is going right and you feel inspired. But what about when you're tired? Unmotivated? Distracted? That's when systems become your greatest ally. They don't rely on mood—they rely on design. Systems keep you moving forward even when you don't feel like it. They help you show up, day in and day out, when motivation is nowhere to be found.

Remember, motivation fades. But systems are built to last.

◇◇◇◇◇

Reflection
Think about a time when motivation wore off. What kept you going—or caused you to stop?

Something to Write About
List one area of your life where you rely too much on motivation. Now write down one system or routine you could put in place to make progress more consistent.

Challenge
Choose one daily task (e.g. journalling, exercise, studying) and build a system around it: same time, same place, same trigger. Stick with it for the next seven days—no exceptions.

Code to Remember
I will build systems that support my growth, even when I don't feel like showing up.

9

Morning Routines & Winning the Day

◇◇◇◇◇

'How you start your day is how you train your mind. Begin with clear intention, and you'll carry that strength into everything else.'

◇◇◇◇◇

Your morning is your first test of the day. And how you handle that first hour—before the world demands your attention—shapes everything that follows. This isn't about waking up at five a.m. or following some influencer's thirty-step routine. It's about ownership. Intention. Leadership.

A strong morning routine isn't a punishment—it's preparation. You're not doing it to impress anyone. You're doing it to show yourself: I lead my life. I don't only just react to it.

Start with something simple. Make your bed. Stretch your body. Breathe deeply. Write down a goal or read something that sharpens your focus. These actions train your mind to stay present and in control, even when life throws distractions or stress your way.

Your morning doesn't need to be perfect to be powerful. It just needs to be yours. Even ten or fifteen minutes of structure can change your mindset for the rest of the day. This is your time to build clarity, calm, and focus before anyone else has a say.

You don't need perfection. You need rhythm. Repetition. Respect for the man you're becoming.

And here's the thing that most people miss: good mornings begin the night before. Your evening habits—what you think, how you unwind, the state of your room—either set you up for momentum or chaos. Knights don't stumble into battle half-asleep. They rise with purpose.

A solid morning routine builds more than discipline—it builds self-trust. It reminds you that your choices have power. That how you start your day is a reflection of how seriously you take your path.

So don't leave it to chance. Set the tone. Build the rhythm. Own your morning—and you'll own your day.

Even a small victory—like getting up on your first alarm or finishing a short workout—can shift your entire mindset. Stack enough of those wins, and you'll start each day in control.

◇◇◇◇◇

💬 Reflection
What's one morning habit that helps me feel grounded and in control?

🎬 Something to Write About
Design a short, realistic morning routine you can actually stick to. Include one thing to move your body and one thing to focus your mind.

⚔ Challenge
Follow your new routine for three days straight. Keep it simple, consistent, and personal to you.

🧭 Code to Remember
I will use my mornings to build focus, discipline, and momentum for the day ahead.

10

Evening Discipline: How You End the Day Matters

◇◇◇◇◇

'You don't rise strong by accident—you prepare for it the night before.'

◇◇◇◇◇

I'm sure you already knew this, but how you end your day is just as important as how you begin it. While mornings set the tone, evenings seal the mindset. The final hour before bed is your chance to slow down, take stock, and prepare for the battles ahead—not just physically, but mentally and emotionally.

Most people waste this time. They zone out, drift through the evening, or stay up too late doing things that drain them instead of build them. But you? You're training to lead yourself. That means ending your day with strength, not surrender.

Evening discipline doesn't have to be complicated. It could mean tidying your space, laying out clothes for tomorrow, reviewing your wins and losses from the day, or setting a clear intention for the next morning. This isn't about a perfect routine—it's about closing your day like someone who respects his time, energy, and mission.

The hours before bed can either ground you or derail you. If you spend your nights scrolling endlessly, avoiding sleep, or letting your thoughts spiral, you're handing away control. But when you use that time to reset—to reflect, to plan, to slow your breathing—you're sharpening your edge for tomorrow.

Good mornings are built the night before. Rest comes easier when your space is calm, your thoughts are clear, and your actions reflect purpose. Momentum builds when your last decision of the day shows discipline—not distraction.

Think of your evening routine as your final act of leadership for the day. You don't need to do it perfectly—you just need to do it on purpose. Set yourself up to rise with clarity instead of chaos.

End your day with intention. Finish strong—so you can start even stronger. Because how you finish today says a lot about how you'll show up tomorrow.

And remember: the man who ends his day in control, grounded and prepared, is already ahead of the one who wakes up scrambling to catch up. Train yourself to be the first.

◇◇◇◇◇

▄ Reflection
How do I usually end my day? Is it helping me or hurting my momentum?

▌ Something to Write About
Create a short evening routine. What two or three actions could help you wind down, reflect, and prepare for a better tomorrow?

✗ Challenge
For the next three nights, stick to your evening routine. Keep it short and consistent. Notice how it changes your mornings.

❷ Code to Remember
I will end my days with discipline—so I can rise with strength and focus.

11

Clean Room. Clear Mind. Strong Focus.

◇◇◇◇◇

'A cluttered room is a cluttered mind. Clean your space, clear your head, and your focus will follow.'

◇◇◇◇◇

Have you ever noticed how much your environment affects your thoughts? When your room is messy and cluttered, it's easy to feel overwhelmed, distracted, and stressed. But when everything is clean and organised, you'll notice that your mind feels clearer, too.

That's not just a coincidence. Your surroundings shape how you think and feel. A chaotic space leads to chaotic thinking. A clean, orderly space creates calm—and that calm gives you strength.

This is why one of the first steps in the journey of self-mastery is cleaning your room. Not because it's a chore, but because it's a declaration. It's a way of saying, I'm taking ownership of my life—starting with what I can control.

Make it a habit. Take time each day to put things back in place. Make your bed. Sweep the floor. Organise your clothes. It doesn't have to be perfect, but it should feel intentional. This is your space. It should reflect the kind of man you're becoming.

When your room is in order, it becomes a place of focus—not frustration. You can think more clearly. You can sit down and do hard things without the nagging feeling something's off. It's not just about comfort—it's about sharpening your discipline.

A clean room doesn't just look better—it helps you feel better. It reminds you that you're in control of your environment, and that mindset carries over into everything else you do. Whether it's school, sport, reading, or rest—you'll show up with more clarity and confidence.

There's a reason many great leaders and thinkers valued tidy, disciplined environments. They understood something powerful: when you command your space, you command your mind.

So don't overlook this. If you want strong focus, start with your room. Clean it. Respect it. Make it a place where your thoughts can grow sharp and your goals can take root.

Clean room. Clear mind. Strong focus. Let it become your standard.

◇◇◇◇◇

💬 Reflection
When have you felt most clear-headed? Was your space tidy or messy? How do you think your environment affects your focus and discipline?

📓 Something to Write About
What does your room look like right now? Does it reflect the man you want to be? What's one small change you could make today?

✕ Challenge
Spend fifteen minutes cleaning your space. Make your bed. Clear the floor. Then pause—does your mind feel sharper?

❷ Code to Remember
I will bring order to my space, so I can bring order to my life.

12

The Discipline of Focus
(Even When You Want to Escape)

⋄⋄⋄⋄⋄

'The men who shape the world are the ones who can stay with a task long after it stops being exciting.'

⋄⋄⋄⋄⋄

There's always something trying to pull you away from the work in front of you. It might be a restless mind, the temptation to wander, or the sudden urge to stretch, snack, scroll, or stare out the window. Distraction doesn't always shout—it whispers. And beneath every whisper is the same thing: the pull to escape discomfort.

It's not wrong to want ease. Everyone does. But if you let that want guide your actions, you'll never build the strength that comes from staying present. You'll avoid discomfort instead of rising through it. And over time, you'll trade your potential for momentary relief.

Focus isn't just about attention. It's about discipline. The kind of discipline that shows up when the work gets repetitive or the silence gets loud. It's a quiet kind of toughness—the ability to remain where you are, doing what matters, even when everything in you wants to move on. That's not natural. It's trained.

You don't need perfect conditions to focus. You don't need total silence, a flawless setup, or the right mood. What you need is practice. You sharpen your ability to stay present by choosing to stay with a task one moment longer. You strengthen your mind every time you resist the urge to quit early, break concentration, or chase comfort.

You teach yourself to keep going when ease would be easier—and that lesson echoes far beyond a single day's task.

That's how men build power—not by jumping from one thing to the next, but by finishing what they started. Over time, this becomes part of your identity: a man who stays when others flinch, who focuses when others fidget, who follows through when others quit.

There's honour in staying the course. There's character in pushing through boredom, discomfort, or challenge without running. The world may never applaud your discipline. You may not get attention or rewards for staying focused. But in the end, it will shape who you are—and that matters far more.

Discipline now. Strength later. It won't be easy, but it will be worth it.

◇◇◇◇◇

▦ Reflection
What kind of discomfort makes you want to quit or turn away from what matters? How do you usually respond when it shows up?

▤ Something to Write About
Describe a time you remained focused even when it was difficult. What did that teach you?

✘ Challenge
Pick a task that needs your focus. Stick with it for thirty minutes without switching. Notice the urge to escape—and stay with it.

❷ Code to Remember
I will train myself to stay, even when everything inside me wants to run.

13

Guard Your Gates (Eyes, Ears, and Heart)

◇◇◇◇◇

'What you let in defines who you become. Guard your eyes, ears, and heart like a fortress. Only let in what strengthens you.'

◇◇◇◇◇

Every day, the world is trying to feed you something—through music, stories, conversations, images, and everything else you take in. And all of it shapes your beliefs, emotions, and decisions. Whether you realise it or not, what you allow into your mind and heart has a powerful influence on your thinking, character, and future.

Your eyes, ears, and heart are gates to your inner world. If you leave them unguarded, anything can walk in and take up space—bitterness, laziness, confusion, negativity, or hate. These forces don't always come crashing in. Sometimes they slip in quietly, through a joke, a habit, a conversation, or even the tone of a story. But once they're in, they begin to shift how you see yourself and the world.

That's why guarding your gates is a form of strength. It's a way of saying, I get to choose what shapes me. And when you're careful about the voices you listen to, the stories you absorb, and the people you surround yourself with, you build a kind of inner armour—one that helps you stay grounded and clear-headed, even when things get loud.

You wouldn't eat junk food every day and expect to feel strong. So why treat your mind any differently? What you feed your thoughts matters just as much as what you feed your body. Choose better inputs. Surround yourself with people who push you to grow. Listen to wisdom that sharpens you. Speak words that build, not break.

Protect your gates not just from what's harmful, but from what's empty. When you fill your mind with things that weaken or waste your focus, you trade strength for ease—and ease never built anything worth keeping.

What you let in shapes what comes out. So guard your gates like a man with something valuable to protect.

◊◊◊◊◊

Reflection
What are some things you've allowed into your mind or heart that left you feeling weaker or more distracted? How have they influenced your thoughts, mood, or behaviour? What would it look like to guard your gates more intentionally?

Something to Write About
Think of three things you regularly take in—songs, stories, conversations, or even environments you spend time in. How does each one affect you afterwards? Do they strengthen your mindset or cloud your focus?

Challenge
Do a twenty-four-hour input audit. Pay close attention to what you allow into your mind through what you hear, see, and engage with. At the end of the day, reflect on what built you up, what wore you down, and what needs to change.

Code to Remember
I will protect my mind and heart by choosing what I allow in.

14

Nobody Becomes a Warrior by Accident

◇◇◇◇◇

'Warriors aren't made by chance—they're forged through discipline, pain, and sacrifice. Don't wait for it to happen. Make it happen.'

◇◇◇◇◇

You know what separates a true warrior from everyone else? It's not talent. It's not luck. It's not a one-time burst of effort. It's consistency.

The greatest warriors aren't born—they're made. They're made through years of hard work, sacrifice, and pushing past their limits. You don't wake up one day and suddenly become strong, courageous, or wise. You become those things by choosing them every single day. Each decision, each challenge you face, and every action you take is what shapes your character and your future.

Think of every choice as a step toward the warrior you want to become. Whether it's staying disciplined, pushing through discomfort, or taking responsibility, each moment is a building block in your journey. Your actions speak louder than words. Becoming a warrior isn't about dreaming—it's about showing up every day. The consistency of your choices will build the man you're becoming.

But you can't do it by accident. Becoming a warrior requires intention, focus, and relentless effort. You can't just hope things will change. You have to actively work on becoming who you want to be. This means embracing discomfort, staying committed when it's a, and refusing to take the easy way out. A warrior doesn't back down. He faces challenges head-on, because he knows every battle is part of the path to greatness.

If you want to be strong, disciplined, and wise, you have to make the decision every day to live like a warrior. There are no shortcuts. There are no easy paths. The warrior's journey is long, gruelling, and filled with sacrifice, but it is the only path that leads to true greatness.

The warrior doesn't look for the easy way out—he chooses the difficult path, again and again, because he knows it's the only way to build lasting strength.

◇◇◇◇◇

▰ Reflection

What does being a 'warrior' mean to you? Consider the traits of a warrior. How can you bring these into your actions today? What specific step can you take to embody this mindset?

▰ Something to Write About

Think about the qualities you admire in a warrior. What traits do you want to develop? Write about how you can work on them and the habits you can cultivate to grow into that man.

✘ Challenge

Pick one habit a warrior would commit to today. It could be waking up earlier, working out, or focusing. Do it with full effort, even if no one notices. Warriors act with discipline, not for recognition—stay committed to your goal.

⊘ Code to Remember

I will train like a warrior—because no one becomes strong by accident.

PART III

Integrity, Truth & Values

What kind of person are you when there's no one to impress? That's where real character is forged—not in the spotlight, but in the quiet moments when only person who knows is you.

This part is about truth: knowing your values, speaking with honesty, and keeping your word even when it's hard. Integrity isn't just about looking good—it's about being solid at the core.

The decisions you make will continue to echo throughout your life, so choose with intention, stand for something, and let your word mean everything.

1

Your Word Is a Sword. Don't Swing It Lightly

◇◇◇◇◇

'A man's word is like a blade. Sharpened by truth. Tempered by honour. And dangerous when used without discipline.'

◇◇◇◇◇

Believe it or not, your words have power—a lot more than you might think. When you speak, you're not just sharing thoughts; you're shaping reality. Another way to look at it is this: your word is a sword. It can build or destroy. It can cut through lies and clear a path for the truth, or it can leave scars that last far longer than you realise.

Keeping your word is absolutely one of the most important things you can ever do. When you say something, you need to mean it—and follow through. Of course, this doesn't mean you should stick to something that puts you in harm's way, hurts another person, or is clearly taking advantage of you. But if you give your word—to help someone, to show up, or to take on a task—it's your responsibility to honour it. This is how you build integrity.

Integrity isn't just doing the right thing when people are watching. It's being the same man when no one is around—when it's just you and your word.

A man who can't be trusted to keep his word has no foundation. And every time you break a promise, you weaken that foundation. You don't just lose the trust of others—you start losing trust in yourself.

As for using your words to wound someone, a man of honour doesn't speak to harm. He doesn't stoop to insults, because he knows how deep those wounds can cut and how quickly they destroy respect. It can be hard—especially when you're angry—but that's when it matters most. Harmful words are remembered far longer than kind ones. They don't just hurt feelings—they leave scars.

Your words should always be a weapon of honour. Sharp enough to cut through distractions, laziness, and dishonesty—but never used to harm others. Like a sword, your word must be wielded with care and responsibility. So the next time you make a promise, or find yourself in a moment where your words carry weight—remember the power they hold.

◇◇◇◇◇

💬 Reflection
When have someone's words stayed with you—good or bad? Why do you think they had that effect?

📓 Something to Write About
Describe a time you gave your word. Did you keep it? What did you learn from the outcome?

⚔ Challenge
This week, mean what you say—and say less when you're angry. Let your word be steady, not sharp.

🧭 Code to Remember
I will speak with honour, follow through on my word, and never use my voice to tear others down.

2

What It Means to Tell the Truth

◇◇◇◇◇

'Telling the truth isn't always easy—but it builds a strength inside you that can't be faked. Only the brave carry the weight of honesty every single day.'

◇◇◇◇◇

Telling the truth is simple in theory, but in practice, it can be a challenge. The truth isn't always the easiest thing to say. It can be uncomfortable, it can hurt, and sometimes it forces you to face parts of yourself you'd rather ignore. But truth is the foundation of everything you will build in life. Without it, your character crumbles, your relationships weaken, and your success is always just out of reach. The truth is a constant anchor, no matter how turbulent the waters around you may become.

Here's something important to understand: The truth is not always what you want to hear—but it's always what you need to hear. It doesn't matter how difficult or inconvenient the truth may be, telling it is a sign of strength, not weakness. It's a sign of character, integrity, and courage. Men who tell the truth live with fewer regrets because they are not burdened by lies or secrets. They don't carry the weight of falsehoods, which only create more problems in the long run.

When you tell the truth, it gives you freedom. It sets you free from the weight of deception and the exhausting pressure to pretend. Lies will always tie you down, hold you back, and eventually reveal themselves. But the truth will lift you up, even when it's demanding. It might not always bring immediate relief, but in the long run, it clears the path to growth, trust, and lasting success.

Now, that doesn't mean you should be brutal or unkind with your truth. Honesty and compassion go hand in hand. You can be truthful without being harsh. You can speak the truth and still show respect for others. And you can hold to your values without needing to shout them at everyone you meet.

Never forget: if you want to grow as a man, you must learn to speak truthfully at all times. It's not just about doing the right thing—it's about becoming the right kind of person. The kind of man whose word can be trusted. The kind of man who doesn't run from the truth—he leads with it.

◇◇◇◇◇

Reflection

What's harder for you—telling the truth to others, or being honest with yourself? Why do you think that is?

Something to Write About

Describe a moment when telling the truth had a cost—but you did it anyway. Or, write about a time you didn't speak the truth, and how that choice affected you or others.

Challenge

Today, pay close attention to your honesty. Catch yourself if you're tempted to twist the truth, exaggerate, or hide something important. Even silent lies count. Choose truth—even if it's uncomfortable.

Code to Remember

I will tell the truth, even when it feels tough—because truth is the foundation of trust.

3

Even When No One Is Watching

◇◇◇◇

'I will choose what's right, even in silence, even in shadows, even when no one else will.'

◇◇◇◇

Integrity, well, real integrity—is what you do when no one is watching. It's easy to make the right choice when others are there to see it—when there's a crowd to cheer you on, a mentor to nod in approval, or a reward waiting on the other side. But real integrity shows up in the quiet, private spaces of your life. It's there when no one is around to notice, when no praise is offered, and when no one but you will ever know what decision you made. In those quiet tests—small and unseen—you prove who you truly are, not just who you appear to be.

That's where your character is built.

You don't need a record to mark every good deed you do. You don't need praise or recognition for every kind act, either. That kind of approval fades quickly anyway. But the way you feel about yourself when you act with honour? That's what truly lasts. It shapes not only how you carry yourself, but how others come to trust you—and how solid your foundation becomes.

The world doesn't need to see you holding the door for someone, picking up litter, or returning money you found on the ground. You don't do those things to be seen—you do them because they're right. That's what separates a man who's pretending from a man who's becoming. One is driven by applause. The other is anchored by values.

There will be moments in life when the easier path is to cut corners, tell a lie, or turn away. And when no one's around, it might seem like you could get away with it. But here's the thing: you're always watching. You have to live with yourself. Every choice you make in silence echoes in your confidence, your peace, and your self-respect.

Be the man who does right—even when it's inconvenient, even when it costs you, even when no one else will ever know. Because that's the man others will come to trust. That's the man you'll be proud to be.

◇◇◇◇◇

💬 Reflection
What do you do when no one is around to see your actions? Are you the same person when no one is looking, or do you act differently?

📓 Something to Write About
Write about a time when you acted with integrity, even though no one would have known if you hadn't. What was the situation, and why did you choose to do the right thing when there was no external pressure to do so?

⚔ Challenge
Today, do something good without expecting anything in return—no recognition, no applause, no praise. Do it simply because it's the right thing to do.

🧭 Code to Remember
I will act with integrity, whether or not anyone is watching—because my character is built on the choices I make when no one is looking.

4

Stand for Something or Fall for Everything

◇◇◇◇◇

'If you don't decide what matters to you, the world will decide for you. And every time you follow the crowd, you lose a little bit of yourself.'

◇◇◇◇◇

Your beliefs and values are your anchor in life. Without them, you're like a ship lost at sea, tossed around by every wave and pushed by every breeze. If you don't know what you stand for, someone else will decide for you. You'll get pulled in by what others think, follow trends that won't last, and try to meet expectations that don't even matter.

When you don't have a clear direction, you'll always feel like you're floating, unsure of where you're going. That's why it's so important to figure out who you are and what matters to you. Here's something I want you to remember: If you stand for nothing, you'll fall for anything.

People who don't know what they believe or where they're headed get swept up in whatever's popular. They end up following the crowd, jumping from one trend to the next, because they don't have something solid to hold on to when things get tough. When things get hard, they'll be easily swayed, never sure of their path.

Now's the time, as a young man, to decide what kind of person you want to be. What principles will you live by? What will you fight for? And just as important, what will you refuse to accept? Draw your line in the sand, and never let anyone push you across it. That line is what shows the world what you won't tolerate—and what you will stand for no matter what.

It's not always easy, and you'll face moments that test you. But when you stand firm in your values, even when no one's watching or when it's tough, you'll earn respect from others. More importantly, you'll earn respect for yourself.

That respect comes from sticking to your word and living by your principles. It becomes the foundation that will keep you grounded when everything else around you changes.

◇◇◇◇◇

💬 Reflection
What do you stand for? What values are you unwilling to compromise on, no matter the situation?

📓 Something to Write About
Think about a time when you compromised on your values or beliefs. What did that cost you? Now, write about a situation where you stood firm, even when it was difficult. How did that make you feel?

⚔ Challenge
Today, identify one area of your life where you've been compromising or wavering. Take a stand. It could be a boundary you've let slide or a value you haven't fully lived by. Stand firm, and let your actions reflect your beliefs.

⊘ Code to Remember
I will stand for something and remain true to my values—because when I stand firm, I build my strength.

5

Strong Enough to Bend, Brave Enough to Stand

◇◇◇◇◇

'A strong man can always admit when he's wrong—but won't fold just to please people. Learn the difference. Both take courage.

◇◇◇◇◇

It's one of the toughest things a man can do: admit when he's wrong. It takes humility, courage, and a deep understanding that we are all fallible. But in the same breath, standing firm when you're right is just as important. Knowing when to apologise and when to stand your ground is the mark of a man who understands integrity. It's about having the wisdom to know the difference and the strength to act accordingly.

When you're wrong, don't let pride get in the way of doing what's right. Apologising is not a sign of weakness, it's a sign of strength. It shows that you are mature enough to accept responsibility and wise enough to learn from your mistakes. A real man doesn't run from his mistakes; he faces them head-on, learns from them, and moves forward stronger. This isn't just about fixing a problem in the moment, but about setting the foundation for growth. Owning your mistakes and learning from them builds a level of maturity that's hard to ignore.

On the flip side, there will be times when you're right, when you know the truth, when your convictions are sound. And in those moments, don't back down. Even if the world pushes against you, even if others question your stance, stand firm in your truth.

Integrity isn't about going with the flow; it's about holding your ground and being strong enough to fight for what's right, even when your back is to the wall. Sometimes, standing tall requires standing alone, and that's where true strength is built.

As you grow, you will find that balance: apologising when necessary and standing your ground when you know you're right. Both are acts of courage and character. They each test different sides of you, but in the end, they make you stronger, more grounded, and more trustworthy. Mastering this balance will define the man you become.

The man who knows when to bend, and when to stand, will earn respect from others—and more importantly, from himself.

◇◇◇◇◇

💬 Reflection
How do you feel when you need to apologise? Is it easy for you, or do you struggle with admitting when you're wrong?

📓 Something to Write About
Write about a time you had to apologise. How did it feel to take responsibility? Then, think of a time you stood firm in your beliefs despite disagreement. How did that boost your confidence?

✘ Challenge
If you owe an apology, give it sincerely, without excuses. If you're sure you're right, stand your ground respectfully and confidently.

◐ Code to Remember
I will apologise when I'm wrong and stand when I'm right—because humility and courage both come from within.

6

The Company You Keep Shapes Your Character

◇◇◇◇◇

'Your character reflects your company—so choose carefully. Who you walk with shapes where you'll end up.'

◇◇◇◇◇

It's been said, 'Show me your friends, and I'll show you your future.' That's not just a clever quote—it's a warning, and a challenge.

The people you spend time with will either pull you upward or drag you down. They'll either water the good in you or slowly poison it. If you walk with fools, don't be surprised when you start thinking like one. But if you surround yourself with men of discipline, courage, and vision, you'll be sharpened by their presence—even if they never say a word. Their habits, their mindset, their drive—these things rub off on you more than you realise.

It's not about thinking you're better than anyone else. It's about being honest: some friendships build your character, others break it down.

Ask yourself:
- Do the people around you push you to grow, or keep you stuck where you are?
- Do they challenge you to be real, or expect you to follow the crowd?
- Do they have your back when it's inconvenient—or only when it benefits them?

Everyone your know influences you in one way or another. And honestly, you become like the people you spend the most time with—whether you see it happening or not. So be deliberate. Choose friends who reflect the kind of man you want to become. Surround yourself with people who hold you to a higher standard, who won't let you quit on yourself, and who won't tolerate you slipping into laziness or excuses.

And remember this: you're not just being shaped—you're shaping others, too. You are someone else's 'company.' What kind of influence are you?

Be the kind of man who sharpens others. Be loyal, real, and committed to growth. The right people will respect it. And over time, you'll build a circle that makes each of you better.

◇◇◇◇◇

💬 Reflection
What does your circle say about you? Do the people around you lift you up—or hold you back?

📓 Something to Write About
Who influences you most right now? Write about someone who makes you better. What makes their impact so strong?

✘ Challenge
Spend time today with people who bring out your best. If someone drags you down, take a step back and check how much influence they really have.

⊘ Code to Remember
I will choose my company wisely—because the people around me will shape the man I become.

7

Don't Lie to Yourself—That's Where It All Starts

⋄⋄⋄⋄⋄

'The moment you stop lying to yourself is the moment you begin to take control of your future.'

⋄⋄⋄⋄⋄

It's easy to lie to yourself. When things get tough, it can feel safer to make excuses or tell yourself that everything will be fine. You convince yourself that you'll change later or that it's not that important. But here's the thing: lying to yourself is the first step in getting stuck. Every time you avoid facing the truth, you build a wall between where you are and where you want to be.

These small lies build up over time. You start brushing things off, telling yourself you've got it under control when you don't. You start ignoring the effort you're not putting in, pretending that your bad habits aren't holding you back. Eventually, you forget what real accountability even looks like. And the more you ignore the truth, the more lost you feel.

It's not just about denying the truth to others—it's about denying it to yourself. And when that happens, you lose trust in your own word. You start second-guessing your decisions, doubting your instincts, and settling for less. You'll begin to accept things that are far below your potential because you've stopped holding yourself to a higher standard.

But when you get real with yourself, everything begins to shift. You stop hiding. You start owning your choices—even the ones that hurt. You face what's not working. You admit what needs to change. And you begin to move forward with clarity and strength.

Being honest with yourself allows you to grow, because growth only happens when you stop pretending. That honesty gives you direction. It sharpens your mind and clears your path.

Once you start telling yourself the truth—no matter how uncomfortable—you'll finally be free to make the changes that matter. You'll earn your own respect. And from there, everything else begins to fall into place.

Don't lie to yourself. That's where it all starts—and where it all can change.

◇◇◇◇◇

💬 Reflection
What's one truth you've been avoiding? Maybe it's a habit you're downplaying or an excuse you keep using. What's one uncomfortable reality you need to face?

📓 Something to Write About
Write about a time you lied to yourself to avoid responsibility. What did it cost you? How might things have gone if you'd been honest from the start?

⚔ Challenge
Ask yourself: What truth am I avoiding right now—about my effort, attitude, or choices? Write it down. Say it out loud. Face it today.

❂ Code to Remember
I will face the truth—even when it's a hard thing to do—because lying to myself is the first step to falling behind.

8

Speak the Truth—But Don't Use It as a Weapon

⋄⋄⋄⋄⋄

'Truth is a really powerful tool, but it can also hurt if used recklessly. Speak with honesty, but always with kindness and respect.'

⋄⋄⋄⋄⋄

Truth is one of the most powerful tools you have, but it's not always easy to wield. You've probably heard the saying, 'The truth hurts,' and while that's often true, the real problem is how we deliver the truth. When you speak the truth, it's essential to do so with care, understanding, and respect. If you speak without thinking, or if your intention is to hurt, you can cause more damage than good.

Speaking the truth can bring clarity and help people grow, but it also requires wisdom. Just because something is true doesn't mean it needs to be said. Sometimes, speaking your mind can seem like the right thing to do, but if it's going to cause unnecessary pain or conflict, it's worth considering whether it's the right time or place. You have to think about how the other person will receive it. Is your truth going to help them, or is it going to make them defensive or hurt their feelings?

It's also important to understand that speaking the truth doesn't always guarantee that it will be accepted or appreciated in the way you intended. Not everyone is ready to hear the truth, and not everyone will agree with you. So, consider your relationship with the person you're speaking to, and make sure your intentions are rooted in care and empathy. If you're trying to help, it will come across in the way you speak.

True strength lies in being able to speak the truth with kindness, even when it's challenging. It's about knowing when to speak and when to stay silent, and it's about using your words to lift others up, not tear them down. When you speak with both honesty and respect, you create a safe space for growth and understanding. It's a reflection of your character, showing that you value the person enough to speak the truth while keeping their dignity intact.

When you speak truthfully and respectfully, you not only help others grow but also grow yourself. It's the cornerstone of building trust and strengthening relationships, something that lasts far beyond a single conversation.

◇◇◇◇◇

▰ Reflection
Think about a time when you told the truth to someone, but it didn't go as you expected. What could you have said differently?

▰ Something to Write About
Write about a time when you had to tell someone a hard truth. How did you say it, and how did they react? What would you change if you could do it again?

✕ Challenge
Today, when you need to speak the truth, think about how your words may affect the other person.

◉ Code to Remember
I will speak the truth with care and respect—because honesty with kindness makes a bigger impact than honesty that hurts.

9

Values Aren't Just Words—They're Lived Every Day

◇◇◇◇◇

'It's easy to talk about values. The real test is living them—your actions show what you truly believe.'

◇◇◇◇◇

Anyone can say they believe in honesty, respect, or hard work. But saying something and living it are two very different things. Your values are not just ideas you talk about—they're the foundation of who you are. If your actions don't match your values, it's like building a house on sand. Eventually, it all falls apart.

It's not what you claim to believe that defines you—it's what you actually do. Living your values means choosing what's right over what's easy. It's telling the truth when lying might save face. It's showing up and doing the work, even when no one's watching. Values become real when they're tested—and you still live by them.

Anyone can talk a good game. But when life punches back, your real character comes through. That's when your values matter most. They guide you when the path isn't clear and help you make choices you won't regret. Anyone can say the right words when life is easy. But it's your actions under pressure that reveal who you are.

So ask yourself: What kind of man do you want to become? What do you stand for when it really counts? Your values are your compass. They help you stay steady when everything else feels like chaos. They won't make every decision easy—but they will make your direction clear.

You won't always live up to your values perfectly. No one does. But if you're honest about where you fall short, and you keep trying to grow, you'll become someone solid. Someone people can rely on. Someone you can be proud of.

Don't let your values just be words. Let them show in your choices, especially when no one's watching. Show them in the way you treat others, how you handle setbacks, and what you stand for when adversity tests you. That's how you build a life of strength and substance.

Because your values shape your character—and your character shapes your future. So don't just talk about them. Live them. Every single day.

◇◇◇◇◇

💬 Reflection
Which of your values is hardest for you to live out consistently? Why do you think that is?

📓 Something to Write About
Write about a time when your actions didn't match the values you say you believe in. How did that moment shape the way you see yourself?

✘ Challenge
Pick one value that matters deeply to you. For the next twenty-four hours, make sure that every decision you make reflects it.

🧭 Code to Remember
I will show what I believe through how I live—because real values are proven, not just spoken.

10

Honour Is Earned, Not Claimed

◇◇◇◇◇

'You don't get honour by saying the right words—you earn it by doing the right things when they're hardest. And once you earn it, no one can take it from you.'

◇◇◇◇◇

Anyone can call themselves 'honourable.' But the truth is, honour isn't something you simply claim—it's something you live. It's not a badge you wear. It's a way you show up every day, especially when no one's around to notice.

Honour is quiet. It's steady. It's built in the moments when you choose to keep your word, protect someone weaker than you, tell the truth even when it stings, and hold yourself to a higher standard—not because someone else demanded it, but because you demanded it of yourself.

There will be people who try to look honourable. They'll talk about loyalty, truth, and courage, but when it really counts, they'll totally disappear, or turn the other way. Real honour isn't loud or self-serving—it's lived.

In every situation, when your actions align with your values, you gain something no one can fake: a reputation that stands the test of time. A man of true honour doesn't need to announce his worth. His actions speak for themselves, and that's what people remember. The measure of your honour isn't in what you say, but in how you act when no one's watching or when things get tough. When you live with integrity, that's the foundation on which honour is built.

And here's another thing: you don't get to decide whether you're honourable. Others will see it in how you treat them and in how you carry yourself, whether it's easy or difficult. Honour is earned in the quiet choices, in the moments when you make the right decision even when no one's keeping score.

In time, if you live with consistency, truth, and care, you'll gain something far more valuable than short-lived praise or fame: you'll gain a name that people trust. That's worth more than money, more than awards, more than anything external. Because when a man's name carries weight, doors open—not just in the world, but within his own soul.

◇◇◇◇◇

💬 Reflection
Do you think people see you as honourable? What do you believe gives a person true honour?

📓 Something to Write About
Write about someone you respect deeply—someone you believe has earned honour. What qualities or actions made you see them that way? Now ask yourself: how can you begin to embody those same traits?

⚔ Challenge
Today, act in a way that earns quiet respect—not attention. Be dependable, honest, and consistent. Let your actions speak louder than your words.

🧭 Code to Remember
I will earn honour through the way I live—not by demanding it, but by deserving it.

11

Integrity Doesn't Shout—It Shows

◇◇◇◇

'Real integrity is invisible. It's in your habits, your choices, and your quiet decisions. It's what you do when no one's around—and it's what makes you trustworthy forever.'

◇◇◇◇

It's easy to look honest when eyes are on you. When there's applause, when people are watching, it feels natural to act kind, be nice, and do the right thing. But as I mentioned back on Day 3, real integrity—the kind that shapes your character and builds a man from the inside out—shows up when no one is watching. That's when it truly matters.

Integrity is more than a set of actions or a way to appear good in front of others. It's about making the right choices when it's inconvenient, uncomfortable, or when there's no one around to see. It's about doing what's right when it's easier to cut corners, take the shortcut, or tell a white lie.

Integrity is choosing discipline when no one would know you slipped. It's telling the truth, even when a lie would protect your image or save you from a difficult conversation. It's about returning the money when the cashier gives you too much change, even if you could easily keep it without anyone noticing. It's how you speak about others when they're not in the room—when there's no audience to impress. Integrity is reflected in the thoughts you entertain, the content you consume, and the decisions you make when you're alone.

In a world that offers a thousand reasons to fake it, integrity stands apart. The man with true integrity doesn't need an audience. He's guided by his inner code—not by external approval or applause. It's not about doing what looks good; it's about doing what's right, even when no one else will see it.

Here's the thing you should understand: integrity builds trust—first from others, and then from yourself. Every time you make the right choice in private, you reinforce your own self-respect. You prove to yourself that your word matters, even when no one else is there to hear it. And that trust, that inner strength, is what sets a man apart.

The world desperately needs men who live with this kind of integrity—men whose actions don't change based on who's watching. The real test of character happens in those quiet, unseen moments.

⋄⋄⋄⋄⋄

💬 Reflection
Think about a recent moment when you had the chance to do the right thing, even though no one was watching. Did you follow through? What does that choice say about your integrity?

📓 Something to Write About
Describe a time when you did the right thing in private—and how it affected the way you saw yourself.

✘ Challenge
Do one good thing today no one will notice. Pick up the rubbish, own a mistake, give full effort. Make that your quiet standard—not a one-off act.

◉ Code to Remember
I will live with quiet integrity—because real strength doesn't need to be seen to be real.

12

Your Reputation Follows Your Choices

⋄⋄⋄⋄

'You can either be liked by everyone, or you can be true to yourself. But you can't do both. Never trade who you are for someone else's approval.'

⋄⋄⋄⋄

It's natural to want to fit in, to feel accepted by the people around you. The desire to belong is part of being human. But too many men, both young and old, fall into the trap of changing who they are just to fit in. They shape their beliefs, actions, and character to match what others expect or want. The problem is, when you change who you are to be liked, you lose a part of yourself. You stop being authentic, and that can lead to a life that feels empty—no matter how many people might approve of you.

The truth of the matter is, the people who matter most in your life will respect you for who you are—not for the version of yourself you pretend to be. When you compromise your soul for the sake of acceptance, you're giving up what makes you unique. You're trading in your authenticity for a fleeting sense of belonging. It's tempting, especially when you're afraid of rejection or judgement, to blend in with the crowd.

But in the long run, the people who truly matter will appreciate you for being real, not for being someone you're not. And if you're pretending, it's only a matter of time before you start to feel disconnected from your true self.

The real challenge is staying true to yourself, even when it's hard. It takes courage to stand firm in your beliefs and values, even when the pressure to conform is strong. But true strength and confidence come from being authentic. When you choose to be yourself, especially in moments of doubt, you start to attract the right people—people who will value and respect you for the person you truly are.

Don't ever give up your values or your identity just to make others like you. You can be yourself, and if someone can't accept that, it's their loss—not yours. When you stand tall in your own truth, you'll find that those who matter most will stick around. Your reputation is built on the choices you make, and staying true to yourself will leave a legacy that lasts.

◇◇◇◇◇

💬 Reflection
Are there any parts of your life right now where you feel like you're pretending to be someone you're not—just to fit in or avoid being judged? What do you think is stopping you from being fully yourself?

📓 Something to Write About
Write about a moment when you changed or hid part of who you really are just to fit in. What did that experience teach you about yourself? Looking back, would you do anything differently?

✗ Challenge
Think of one area where you've been holding back to stay accepted. Today, choose honesty. Show who you really are—even if it feels risky.

❷ Code to Remember
I will stay true to myself, because no acceptance is worth the cost of losing who I am.

13

Live What You Believe, Even When It's Hard to Do

'Anyone can do the right thing when it's easy. It's when it costs you—when it's risky or uncomfortable—that you find out what kind of man you really are.'

Doing what's right is easy when there's no cost. When nobody's watching, when the stakes are low, and when the choice is obvious—it barely feels like a decision at all.

But what about when doing what's right becomes hard to do? When doing the right thing means losing popularity, being laughed at, standing alone, or even facing real consequences? That's when your values stop being ideas and start becoming choices.

You'll face moments in life where your beliefs will be tested. Maybe someone asks you to lie to protect them. Maybe your friends are doing something shady and want you to join in. Maybe telling the truth means facing embarrassment, discipline, or losing something you care about. These moments are uncomfortable—but they're also defining. They separate the ones who just talk about integrity from the ones who actually live it.

A man of character doesn't just follow the crowd. He doesn't bend his standards to fit in. He stands firm, even if it means standing alone. He knows that doing what's right might cost him something in the moment—but it's always worth it in the long run.

Doing the right thing might not bring instant rewards. You might not get praised. You might even feel misunderstood. But every time you act with honesty, courage, and conviction, you're building something far more valuable than approval—you're building self-respect. And when you respect yourself, everything else changes. Your confidence grows. Your reputation builds. And slowly, the world starts to see you as someone they can count on.

You won't get it right every time. No one ever does. But each time you choose what's right over what's easy, you grow stronger. And over time, those small but courageous decisions shape the kind of man you become—a man who lives what he believes, even when it feels like an uphill battle.

That's how a legacy is built. One decision at a time.

◇◇◇◇◇

▣ Reflection
What stops you from doing the right thing when the pressure is high or when the consequences feel too heavy?

📓 Something to Write About
Write about a moment when you knew what the right thing to do was—but doing it came at a cost. What did you choose, and how do you feel about that decision now?

✗ Challenge
Today, choose to do the right thing, especially if it's uncomfortable. Own your mistake, helping someone no one else notices, or speak up when silence feels safer.

● Code to Remember
I will do the right thing—even when it's hard to do—because that's how real strength is built.

14

Your Conscience Is Your Compass

◇◇◇◇◇

'There's a quiet voice in you that already knows what's right. It doesn't shout—but it guides. Listen to it long enough, and it becomes your compass for life.'

◇◇◇◇◇

Every man has a conscience—a built-in compass pointing him toward what's right. It's not loud. It doesn't demand your attention. But it knows. And if you learn to listen to it, it will steer you straight.

Sometimes it shows up as a quiet whisper—when you're tempted to lie, when you know you should apologise, when you're thinking about following the crowd just to fit in. Other times, it roars in your chest, pulling hard against a decision that would cost you your integrity. Either way, the signal is there. The question is whether you'll listen.

Your conscience isn't always perfect. Like anything else, it can be shaped—for better or worse. That's why you train it. Just like your body needs exercise and your mind needs challenges, your moral compass needs sharpening. Feed it truth. Take time to reflect. Keep good men around you—men who aren't afraid to challenge you. Ask questions. Wrestle with what you believe. Every time you act on your conscience, you make it a little clearer, a little stronger.

But if you ignore it long enough, it fades. It doesn't disappear—but it gets quieter. You stop noticing the nudge. You stop feeling the tension. That's when you risk losing your way. You might still look disciplined or successful on the outside—but inside, you'll feel dis connected. Hollow.

That's why your conscience matters. It's not there to make life easier. It's there to help you live well. It's the part of you that points to the man you're meant to become.

So tend to it (garden, remember?). Protect it. Trust it when it speaks—even when it challenges you. Because a man who honours his conscience, even when it costs him, is a man who can live with himself. And that kind of peace is worth more than praise or approval. It's the quiet strength of a life well lived.

◇◇◇◇◇

▣ Reflection
When was the last time your conscience warned you about something—but you chose to ignore it? What happened as a result, and what do you think that moment taught you?

▤ Something to Write About
Write about a time when you followed your conscience, even though it would've been easier not to. What did you decide to do, why did you choose that path, and how did it feel afterwards?

✘ Challenge
Today, make an effort to really listen to your inner compass. If you're faced with a decision—even a small one—pause and ask yourself what choice lines up with your values. Then follow through, even if it's not the easiest option.

❷ Code to Remember
I will follow my conscience, even when it costs me—because that's how I stay true to myself.

PART IV

Brotherhood & Role Models

Knights aren't meant to journey alone. The men you walk with will either sharpen you or dull your edge.

This part is about choosing your circle wisely—spotting real loyalty, building unshakeable trust, and becoming the kind of brother others can rely on.

Being part of a Brotherhood isn't just about friendship—it's about accountability, shared values, and having each other's backs when it matters most.

The right men in your circle won't just support your growth—they'll challenge you to rise.

1

Choose Friends Who Sharpen You

⋄⋄⋄⋄⋄

'The people closest to you will shape the man you become—so choose the ones who make you sharper, not softer.'

⋄⋄⋄⋄⋄

As you'll undoubtedly find out over time, an important decision you'll ever make in life is who you allow to be close to you. The people you spend time with will shape your future more than you think. Your mindset, your habits, and even your character are all influenced by your inner circle. The right friends can push you forward. The wrong ones can hold you back or lead you down a path you'll regret.

There's a huge difference between friends who are just around for fun, and friends who sharpen you. The second kind—the rare kind—are the ones who push you to improve, who hold you accountable, and who want to see you win. They won't just hype you up when it's easy—they'll call you out when you're off track, and stand by you when things fall apart. These aren't just friends. They're brothers.

There's an old saying: Iron sharpens iron. Just like metal is made sharper through friction, men are sharpened through challenge. That friction isn't always comfortable, but it's necessary. Real growth doesn't happen in comfort zones—it happens when you're stretched, challenged, and surrounded by those who bring out the best in you.

The goal isn't to collect a crowd. It's to build a circle that strengthens you. One solid friend who pushes you to grow is worth more than ten who keep you stuck. Think about it—who are the voices you hear most often? Who are the people influencing your decisions, even without you realising it?

Ask yourself honestly: Are your friends helping you rise or making it easier to settle? Do they push you toward discipline, respect, and purpose—or do they pull you toward distractions, excuses, and shortcuts?

Surround yourself with men who remind you of your potential. Choose friends who don't just make you laugh, but make you better. That's the kind of brotherhood that builds strong men.

◇◇◇◇◇

▧ Reflection
What kind of impact do your closest friends have on your mindset, your habits, and your growth?

🗒 Something to Write About
Write about one friend who genuinely challenges you to be better. What qualities do they have that sharpen you—and how can you be that kind of friend to someone else?

✘ Challenge
Spend more time this week with someone who brings out the best in you. Notice how you feel after hanging out—energised or drained. Then act accordingly.

❷ Code to Remember
I will surround myself with those who make me sharper, not smaller.

2

The Brotherhood Test: Are They for You or Themselves?

'A real brother stands with you when it costs him something. The fake ones disappear when it no longer benefits them.'

When it comes to brotherhood, one of the most important lessons you'll ever learn is how to recognise whether the men around you are truly for you—or simply in it for themselves. This can be hard to see at first. Some people are good at putting on a mask and playing the part. But over time, patterns reveal character. Watch closely, and their actions will tell you everything you need to know if you're paying attention.

A real brother is someone who wants to see you win—especially when there's nothing in it for him. He celebrates your growth, not because it makes him look good, but because he genuinely wants what's best for you. He offers support when you're struggling, encouragement when you're doubting yourself, and truth when you're slipping. He doesn't compete with you—he builds with you. He's not threatened by your progress; he's inspired by it.

A selfish friend, on the other hand, will make it all about him. He might act supportive until you start doing better than him. Then the jealousy kicks in. He might only reach out when he needs something or disappear the moment things get hard. These kinds of friendships are shallow. They're built on convenience, not commitment, and they tend to crumble when pressure hits.

It's easy to be fooled by shared interests or good times. But brotherhood goes far deeper than that. Real brotherhood is tested in the storms. It's forged through challenge, trust, honesty, and time. You need people around you who are solid when life isn't. Friends who are more invested in who you're becoming than in what they can get from you.

Ask yourself: Do your friends lift you when you're low—or do they vanish? Do they challenge you when you're off course—or stay quiet to keep things easy? Are they giving more than they take?

True brotherhood isn't measured by how well you get along—it's measured by how much you push each other to grow. Stand with men who challenge you, strengthen you, and stay loyal when it matters most. That's the kind of bond that lasts.

◇◇◇◇◇

🔲 Reflection
Have you ever had a friend who only came around when they needed something? What did that teach you about loyalty?

📓 Something to Write About
List the qualities that define a loyal friend. Then ask yourself—do your current friends reflect these qualities? Do you?

✘ Challenge
Pay attention this week to how your friends respond when you succeed—or when you struggle. True brotherhood shows itself in both moments.

⊘ Code to Remember
I will build my circle with those who show up, not just speak up.

3

Learn from Those Who've Walked Ahead

◇◇◇◇◇

'Not every man is a role model. But every man can teach you something—if you're paying attention.'

◇◇◇◇◇

You don't have to figure it all out alone. There are men who've already walked this road—who've taken wrong turns, fallen hard, gotten back up, and come away with wisdom that can save you time and pain. Learn early what they learnt late. That's not weakness. That's wisdom. And if you're smart, you'll take full advantage of it.

Some of these men might be your father. Others might be coaches, teachers, mentors, or older friends who've earned their stripes through experience. A father—by blood or bond—is often the first man to show you what strength, responsibility, and perseverance look like up close. If he's present in your life, pay attention. Not just to his victories, but to his mistakes too. Watch how he handles stress. Notice how he treats people. Learn from both what he gets right and where he falls short.

And if you don't have that kind of figure in your life, don't use that as your excuse. That's your mission. Find one. Look for men who carry themselves with discipline, honour, and humility. Men who are walking in the direction you want your life to go. They're out there—but you have to be intentional about finding them.

You don't need perfect role models. You need real ones. Men with scars and stories. You don't need to copy everything they do—just watch closely. Some will show you who to become. Others, who not to become. Either way, if you're paying attention, you're gaining ground.

Mentorship doesn't always come wrapped in a formal conversation. Sometimes, it's just observation. How a man carries himself under pressure. How he handles failure without quitting. How he speaks about others when they're not around. That can teach you more than a lecture ever could.

And when one of them does take the time to speak into your life—listen. Don't just nod. Let it sink in. Let it shape you.

You're not meant to do this journey alone. But you are responsible for who you choose to learn from. So choose men worth learning from.

◇◇◇◇◇

💬 Reflection
Who is one man—past or present—you've learnt from just by watching him? What stuck with you?

📓 Something to Write About
What did you learn from an older man—without him saying a word? How did it shape how you see manhood?

✖ Challenge
This week, choose one man you respect. Write down three things about him you'd want to carry into your own life.

◎ Code to Remember
I'll pay attention to the men ahead of me—and take the lessons they leave behind.

4

You'll Outgrow Some People— And That's Okay

◇◇◇◇◇

'Growth will cost you certain friendships. If they're meant to go with you, they'll rise with you.'

◇◇◇◇◇

As you move through life, you'll notice something that might feel strange at first—you start to outgrow some people. Friends you were once tight with may feel distant. You might not laugh at the same things anymore. You might want more out of life while they stay the same. It can feel like a loss, especially if you've shared a lot of memories. You might even feel guilty for drifting apart.

But outgrowing people isn't necessarily a bad thing. It's a natural part of growth, even if uncomfortable at first.

Not every friendship or relationship is meant to last forever. Whether that's a few months or several years, as you develop your values, interests, and ambitions, you may find the people you once connected with no longer share the same vision for their lives.

As you figure out your values, goals, and direction, you'll start noticing who's aligned with that and who isn't. It doesn't mean they're bad people. It just means they're not growing in the same way—or at the same pace—as you are.

If you hold on to every old friendship out of guilt, comfort, or fear of change, you risk slowing yourself down. Growth takes focus, and sometimes that means letting go of relationships that no longer fit the path you're walking. It might feel uncomfortable at first, but that space you're clearing? That's where new people will show up—people who match your mindset, drive, and vision for the future.

Letting go doesn't mean you stop caring. It means you care enough about your future to choose what's best for you. The right people will walk with you, while the others may fall behind—and that's okay. It's part of the process.

You're not the same person you were last year, and that's the point. Growth changes things, sometimes in unexpected ways. And one of the biggest signs you're becoming the man you're meant to be is when you realise it's time to move forward—even if not everyone comes with you.

Outgrowing people isn't failure. It's progress. Keep moving forward. You're allowed to grow.

◇◇◇◇◇

▰ Reflection
Why do you think some friendships fade over time? Is it always a bad thing—or can it sometimes mean you're growing?

▰ Something to Write About
Write about a friendship you've outgrown. What changed? Did holding on help or hinder your growth?

✘ Challenge
Be honest about who's growing with you—and who's holding you back. Choose how close they stay. Protect your momentum.

◉ Code to Remember
I will not hold myself back just to stay where I no longer belong. I will keep moving forward.

5

You're Not Meant to Walk Your Path Alone

'Even the strongest warrior needs a tribe. Isolation doesn't make you tougher—it makes you weaker.'

Another one of the most important things you'll learn in life is that you are not meant to go about it alone. As men, we are built for connection, for community. We thrive when we're part of something greater than ourselves, especially within brotherhood. There will be times when you need to stand alone, but the strength to do that comes from knowing that you have a solid foundation of brothers who've got your back.

This idea of brotherhood isn't just about having a group of people around to pass the time or share surface-level experiences. It's about building relationships based on mutual respect, trust, and genuine support. A true brotherhood is a place where men challenge each other to grow, where they offer real support during tough times, and where they hold each other accountable to the standards they've set for themselves. Brotherhood means being able to rely on one another when it counts the most.

You might find yourself in a time of transition, or maybe you'll face a situation that makes you feel like you have to walk the path alone. But this is where brotherhood becomes most essential. Lean into it. There are men who have walked similar paths and are ready to share their wisdom. And just as you seek their guidance, there will be others who need you to be that source of strength. Brotherhood is about helping each other, and in doing so, you'll grow stronger together.

Having a strong brotherhood doesn't mean you won't face difficulties on your own; it means you'll never have to bear them completely alone. Even when you stand tall on your own, the knowledge that you have brothers behind you makes all the difference. So seek out those who will challenge you, who will sharpen you, and be the brother who sharpens others.

The path may not always be easy, but with a true brotherhood, you'll always have the strength to walk it.

◇◇◇◇◇

💬 Reflection
When have you felt most isolated—and what did you learn from that experience?

📓 Something to Write About
Describe a moment when you reached out for help or leaned on someone else. What stopped you at first? What changed when you did?

⚔ Challenge
This week, start a real conversation with someone you trust. Don't just talk about surface things—check in, open up, and offer the same in return.

🧭 Code to Remember
I will build strong connections—because strength isn't built in silence or solitude.

6

Help Others Without Expecting Anything Back

◇◇◇◇◇

'When you help your brother without keeping score, you both rise. That's what honour looks like.

◇◇◇◇◇

Helping others without expecting something back is a mark of a man who leads with strength. In a world where so many relationships are built on give-and-take, it's easy to fall into the trap of thinking that help, support, or even friendship must come with strings attached. However, true brotherhood operates on a different principle—selflessness. Real men don't approach relationships with the expectation of getting something back. They help because it's the right thing to do.

When you step up to help someone, do it out of a genuine desire to see them succeed, grow, or overcome their challenges. Help without waiting for recognition, favours, or anything in return. This doesn't mean you should let yourself be walked over or taken advantage of. It's about knowing your worth and setting boundaries, while still giving freely and helping others simply because you want to see them rise.

The strength of a true brotherhood is found in this generosity. When men come together to support one another with no expectation of something in return, they create a bond that is unshakeable. The act of giving and helping, without ulterior motives, creates a depth of trust and respect that can't be easily broken. In the process, it not only strengthens the brotherhood, but it also builds your own character.

Helping others teaches you humility, patience, generosity, and the deep satisfaction that comes from lifting those around you.

Remember, real men don't help because they expect something in return—they help because it's the right thing to do. They understand that true strength is found in lifting others, and that helping others grow and succeed is what builds their own foundation of strength.

So be the kind of man who offers help freely, without conditions or expectations—but also with the wisdom to protect yourself. That's how you build true, lasting brotherhood—and how you grow into the man you're meant to be.

◇◇◇◇◇

💬 Reflection
Have you ever helped someone without expecting anything back? How did it feel?

📓 Something to Write About
Write about a time someone helped you with no strings attached. What impact did it have on you—and what did it teach you about real brotherhood?

✘ Challenge
Do something this week for someone else with no expectation of recognition, payback, or applause. Let it be enough to know you showed up.

❷ Code to Remember
I will give without keeping score—because brotherhood isn't a transaction.

7

Role Models Aren't Perfect, But They're Real

⋄⋄⋄⋄⋄

'Don't wait for flawless mentors—follow the ones who've been through the fire and came out stronger.'

⋄⋄⋄⋄⋄

It's easy to put people on pedestals—to think that a role model has to be flawless, always right, or somehow better than you. But the thing is, real role models aren't perfect. And they don't have to be. In fact, it's their imperfections, their honesty about their struggles, and the way they handle failure that make them truly worth looking up to.

When you're growing into the man you're meant to be, you'll start looking for examples—men who live with purpose, stand by their values, and keep moving forward even when life throws setbacks their way. These are the men who inspire you not because they've never fallen, but because they get back up and keep going. They own their mistakes, learn from them, and keep building themselves day by day. That's real strength.

Don't waste time searching for the 'perfect' role model. Instead, look for men who live with integrity—men who are doing the work, leading by example, and walking the kind of path you want to walk. They won't have all the answers, but they'll show you what it means to keep learning, growing, and showing up. A real role model doesn't pretend to be invincible. He shows you that discipline, resilience, and courage are built—not inherited.

And remember, one day, you'll be that example for someone else. You don't need to have it all figured out to be a role model. You just need to be honest about where you're at, committed to growth, and willing to walk with purpose. Someone younger or earlier in their journey will look at the way you carry yourself, how you treat others, how you handle pressure—and they'll learn from that.

Role models don't need to be larger than life. They just need to be real. The kind of man who chooses progress over perfection and keeps showing up, day after day.

Look for those men. Learn from them. And become one of them. You never know who's watching—or who's counting on you to lead the way.

⬦⬦⬦⬦⬦

▦ Reflection
What qualities do you admire most in the men you look up to—and why?

▮ Something to Write About
Think of a role model in your life who wasn't perfect, but who still impacted you. What did you learn from his flaws, not just his strengths?

✕ Challenge
This week, stop looking for perfect examples. Choose one man in your life you can learn from—and start paying attention to how he handles pressure, failure, and growth.

◉ Code to Remember
I will follow men who are real—not flawless—because growth leaves scars.

8

The Strength in Vulnerability

'There's significantly more strength in saying 'I need help' than in pretending you don't need it at all.'

In a world that often prizes toughness, vulnerability can seem like a weakness. From a young age, many men are taught to hide their emotions—keep a stiff upper lip, never cry, never complain. The message is clear: strength means staying silent, pushing through, and never showing cracks. But that mindset builds walls, not strength.

Honestly speaking, real strength is the ability to be honest—especially about the things that hurt. Vulnerability isn't about falling apart or being soft. It's about being brave enough to say, 'I'm not okay right now.' It's about owning your story, even the parts that aren't polished or easy to talk about.

When you open up, you don't make yourself smaller—you make space for connection. That's where real brotherhood begins. Not in shared victories, but in shared struggles. When you're willing to be seen in your lowest moments, and when others show up for you in that space, something powerful happens: trust grows. Bonds deepen. You realise you're not alone in your battles.

Vulnerability is also a gateway to growth. When you pretend everything's fine, you're not just lying to others—you're lying to yourself. That kind of denial slows your progress. But when you face your fears, speak your truth, and ask for help when you need it, you start moving forward. You start healing. You start becoming a man who isn't ruled by what he's afraid to feel.

Of course, vulnerability doesn't mean dumping your emotions on everyone you meet. It means choosing the right moments—and the right people—to be real with. It means building relationships where honesty is respected and mutual. It's not about being dramatic. It's about being human.

So if you feel broken, confused, or overwhelmed—speak up. Reach out. Let someone in. That's not weakness. That's courage.

The strongest men are the ones who show up fully, even when they're hurting. Vulnerability isn't the opposite of strength—it's what gives strength its depth.

◇◇◇◇◇

💬 Reflection
Why do you think many men struggle to open up emotionally? Have you ever felt that pressure yourself?

🎬 Something to Write About
Write about a moment when you were honest about something difficult. How did the people around you respond? How did you feel afterwards?

⚔ Challenge
Choose one person you trust and open up about something real. It doesn't have to be dramatic—just true. Watch what happens when you lead with honesty instead of hiding.

🎖 Code to Remember
I will be brave enough to speak the truth—even when my voice shakes.

9

Stand by Your Brothers, Even When It's Hard to Do

◇◇◇◇

'Loyalty isn't about convenience. It's about showing up when it demands more than you feel like giving.'

◇◇◇◇

True brotherhood isn't measured by how often you laugh together, but by how deeply you stand together—especially when things get hard. It's easy to be there when life feels light, when everything is going well and success is flowing. But the real test of loyalty is what you do when your brother is struggling, hurting, or falling behind.

Standing by someone in their darkest moments takes grit. It's not always convenient. Sometimes it's messy, uncomfortable, and even frustrating. But brotherhood was never meant to be built on comfort—it's meant to be built on commitment. Real men don't disappear when things get hard. They lean in.

Being that kind of friend doesn't mean you always have the right words or the perfect solution. Often, it's not about fixing the problem. It's about showing up. Being present. Letting your brother know, 'I see you. I'm here. You're not alone.' That kind of presence can carry more weight than advice ever could.

At times, standing by your brothers will stretch you. It might mean sacrificing your time, energy, or even putting your own needs second for a moment. It might mean speaking hard truths or offering support when you don't fully understand the situation. But that's what loyalty looks like in action—it's not always clean, but it's always real.

An important truth to remember is: the way you show up for others becomes the foundation of the relationships that will one day carry you. When your time of struggle comes—and it will—you'll want to know there are men around you who won't flinch, who won't fade away when things get complicated.

Don't just be a fair-weather friend. Be the brother who shows up when it counts. The brother who stays. The brother who listens, who helps, who walks through the fire beside someone else—even when it would be easier to walk away.

That's the kind of loyalty that turns friendships into something far more powerful. That's brotherhood forged in truth.

◇◇◇◇◇

💬 Reflection
When someone you care about is struggling, do you lean in—or pull away?

📓 Something to Write About
Think about a time someone in your life was going through a rough patch. Did you show up for them? If not, what stopped you? If you did, what did it teach you?

✘ Challenge
Reach out to a friend or brother who's been quiet or distant. Let them know you're there—especially if it feels a little uncomfortable.

⊘ Code to Remember
I will stand beside my brothers—even when silence would be easier.

10

Build a Brotherhood Based on Growth, Not Just Fun

◇◇◇◇

'Friendships built solely on fun may crack under pressure. But brotherhoods forged in growth, grit, and purpose will endure anything.'

◇◇◇◇

It's easy to build friendships around shared interests like sports, music, games, or just passing time together. And while there's nothing wrong with having fun, true brotherhood runs deeper than laughter and casual connection. A lasting brotherhood is built on shared values, personal growth, and a commitment to helping one another become better men.

The strongest bonds are forged not in moments of comfort, but in times of challenge and change. Brothers who are serious about growth will challenge you—not to tear you down, but to build you up. They won't let you stay stuck in bad habits, and they won't stand by while you sabotage your own potential. They'll push you to rise. And you'll push them in return.

This kind of brotherhood creates something rare—accountability that comes from trust. When your brothers believe in who you can become, they'll expect more from you. They'll call you out when you fall short, and they'll be there to pick you up when you're struggling. It's not about judgement—it's about helping each other live with discipline, purpose, and integrity.

You'll also find that a brotherhood rooted in growth leads to shared victories that mean more. When you and your brothers work through hardship, support each other through failure, and celebrate hard-earned wins, the bond becomes stronger than anything built on surface-level fun alone.

But growth-based brotherhood isn't always easy. It requires effort. It takes honesty, humility, and a willingness to be uncomfortable. You'll need to open up, speak truthfully, and be willing to both give and receive feedback. That kind of connection takes time—but it's worth it.

Don't settle for shallow friendships. Build a brotherhood that sharpens you, challenges you, and grows with you. Seek out guys who are serious about becoming more—and become that kind of guy yourself. Together, you'll become stronger than you ever could alone. That's the kind of brotherhood that lasts. That's the kind that changes lives.

◇◇◇◇◇

▪ Reflection
Who in your life challenges you to grow—not just laugh or waste time?

▪ Something to Write About
Write about the difference between friends who distract you and friends who push you forward. Which group have you spent more time with lately?

✘ Challenge
Initiate a real conversation this week—not about games, gossip, or drama, but about goals, struggles, and growth.

● Code to Remember
I will choose brotherhood that builds me—not just entertains me.

11

Find Your Tribe—And Keep It Tight

⋄⋄⋄⋄⋄

'Brotherhood isn't about having a crowd. It's about having a core.'

⋄⋄⋄⋄⋄

As you journey through life, you'll cross paths with many people. Some will come and go without leaving much behind. But a rare few will truly see you—your strengths, your flaws, your potential—and challenge you to grow. These men are your tribe. They're not just friends or acquaintances. They're your brothers, bound not by blood, but by values, loyalty, and shared purpose.

It's important to understand that your tribe isn't about how many people surround you. It's about depth, not numbers. A strong tribe is built on quiet consistency, not loud popularity. It's formed through trust earned over time, through challenges faced side by side, and through a shared commitment to becoming better men together.

The right tribe sharpens you. They hold you accountable when you're slipping, encourage you when you're doubting yourself, and remind you of your worth when you forget it. They don't let you settle for less than you're capable of. These are the men who show up—not just when it's convenient, but when you need them the most. They celebrate your wins as if they were their own, and they stand beside you in the storms. They speak truth, not just comfort. They listen, not just wait to speak. And most importantly, they live what they say—they don't just talk about loyalty, integrity, or growth. They live it, daily.

Once you find these men, protect that bond. Keep your circle tight. Don't open the door to people who drain your energy, gossip behind your back, or envy your progress. Be discerning. The strength of your tribe will shape the strength of your future.

Brotherhood like this doesn't happen by accident—it's built with intention. Choose your tribe wisely. Then be that kind of man for others. Be someone they can trust, lean on, and grow beside. When you commit to that, you'll find that your tribe becomes one of the greatest assets in your life—and one of the clearest reflections of the man you're becoming.

◇◇◇◇◇

▰ Reflection
Who are the people in your life that actually make you better—not just more comfortable?

🎞 Something to Write About
List the names of the three people who most challenge and support your growth. What makes those relationships different from the rest?

✗ Challenge
Start acting like your tribe matters. Spend more time with the ones who sharpen you. Let go of the ones who only stick around when it's easy.

❷ Code to Remember
I will build and stand with a brotherhood that sharpens me—and protect it like it matters.

12

The Strength in Openness: Building Real Brotherhood

◇◇◇◇

'Brothers don't just stand side by side in the good times—they face the storm together.'

◇◇◇◇

In a world where strength is often mistaken for silence and emotional distance, vulnerability can seem like a weakness. Men are taught to keep things bottled up, to 'tough it out,' and to never show pain. But real strength isn't about holding everything in—it's about the courage to be open and honest with your brothers. Vulnerability means sharing the real you—your struggles, your fears, your doubts—and trusting others enough to see behind the armour.

When you open up, you create a space where others can do the same. That's where real brotherhood begins. It's not just about sharing laughs or victories—it's about being there for each other when life gets hard. Brotherhood that only shows up during the fun moments won't last. But brotherhood rooted in truth, built on the willingness to be seen and to see others clearly—that kind of connection is rare, and powerful.

True strength isn't about suppressing your emotions or pretending you're fine when you're not. It's about recognising that courage and honesty go hand in hand. When you speak the truth about what you're going through, you give your brothers permission to do the same. That creates a deeper connection, one based on respect, not appearances.

It's not always easy. Opening up takes guts. It might feel uncomfortable or unfamiliar, especially if you've spent years trying to handle everything on your own. But over time, you'll find that openness doesn't weaken your relationships—it strengthens them.

Real brotherhood isn't built on silence, distance, or pretending everything is okay. It's built on trust, and trust is earned through honesty, consistency, and vulnerability. You don't have to share everything with everyone—but with your tribe, you should be able to speak your truth without fear of judgement.

When you commit to being open, you help build a brotherhood that can't be shaken—one that lifts each other up, holds each other accountable, and never leaves a man behind.

◇◇◇◇◇

▣ Reflection
Recall a time you opened up to a brother. How did it affect your bond? What did you learn about yourself?

▪ Something to Write About
Describe a moment you held something back. Why didn't you share it? What might've changed if you had?

✘ Challenge
Share something real with a brother this week. It doesn't have to be deep—just honest. Pay attention to how it changes the connection.

◉ Code to Remember
I will show courage and honesty, knowing it strengthens my brotherhood. True strength lies in speaking the truth when it would be easier to say nothing.

13

Don't Just Follow—Lead When It's Your Turn

◇◇◇◇◇

'Leadership is never about taking control, it's about taking responsibility and guiding others to rise with you.'

◇◇◇◇◇

Leadership isn't a title—it's an action. True leaders rise when there's a need, whether they're in the spotlight or standing quietly in the background. Leadership is about stepping up when others are uncertain, when a decision needs to be made, or when the group needs direction. It's about doing what's right—even when it's unpopular, uncomfortable, or costly—and thinking beyond yourself. Real leaders don't wait for permission—they lead by example, through courage, consistency, and integrity.

Being a leader doesn't mean you always have to be the loudest voice or the one giving orders. In fact, some of the best leaders are the ones who know when to speak up and when to listen. They know how to lift others up, bring out the best in their brothers, and keep the group focused on something greater than just the moment. It's not about being in control—it's about being responsible. And that responsibility starts with leading yourself first.

You don't have to know everything to lead. No one does. But what you *do* need is the willingness to try, to learn, and to take ownership of your actions. That's what earns respect—not perfection, but character. People follow leaders who are real, who stay steady in difficult times, and who care more about doing what's right than looking impressive.

Leadership will show up in your life in many different forms—sometimes at school, sometimes in your friendships, and later in your work, family, or community. You won't always expect it, but when that moment comes, take it. Step forward. Set the tone. Show your brothers what it means to lead with strength and humility.

When you choose to lead with purpose, others will follow—not because they have to, but because they believe in you. And that kind of leadership changes lives.

◇◇◇◇◇

▰ Reflection
Have you ever been in a situation where you needed to step up and lead, but hesitated? What held you back, and how did it impact the situation?

▰ Something to Write About
Write about a time when you had to make a tough decision for the good of the group. What was the decision, how did you handle it, and what did you learn from the experience?

✗ Challenge
Take notice of a situation where leadership is needed—whether in your friendships, work, or personal life. Step up and make a decision, even if it feels uncomfortable. Lead with confidence and humility, and reflect on how it affects those around you.

◉ Code to Remember
I will step up when my time comes to lead, guiding others with confidence and humility, knowing that real leadership elevates those around me.

14

True Brotherhood Doesn't Compete—It Elevates

◇◇◇◇◇

'The strength of a true brotherhood isn't measured by who stands tallest—but by how many stand together.'

◇◇◇◇◇

In a true brotherhood, there's no room for envy, pride, or one-upmanship. It's not a race to outshine each other—it's a commitment to raise each other higher. When one man achieves something great, it's not a threat to the others; it's a reason to celebrate. His victory is a reminder of what's possible. Real brothers don't compete for the spotlight—they share it. They understand that the strength of the group depends on how well each man is supported, challenged, and encouraged to grow.

Brotherhood is a place where iron sharpens iron. Each man pushes the others to be better—not for ego, but for the good of the whole. When one man struggles, the rest don't turn away. They step in. They steady him, lift him, and remind him of who he is. The wins and losses aren't isolated—they're shared, carried together, and learnt from as a unit.

This kind of bond isn't formed by accident. It's built intentionally, through trust, accountability, and a shared standard. In that space, competition fades. The measure of a man isn't how far ahead he gets, but how well he helps those beside him move forward too. True brotherhood means that no man is left behind—not because he's weak, but because we're stronger together.

When every member of a brotherhood is committed to each other's rise, something powerful happens. The group becomes more than the sum of its parts. Each success adds strength. Each challenge becomes an opportunity to close ranks and grow tighter. A true brother is one who shows up—not just when it's easy, but when it requires patience, grit, and humility.

In the end, brotherhood isn't about comparison—it's about contribution. Not who stands tallest, but who stands together. Because the real goal isn't to beat one another—it's to build something lasting. And that kind of strength doesn't come from competition. It comes from honour, sacrifice, and the unshakeable decision to rise... together.

◇◇◇◇◇

▰ Reflection
Have you ever felt threatened by someone else's success? What if their win helped both of you? How can you start seeing your brothers' progress as strength for all?

▰ Something to Write About
Think of a time when someone's success made you feel jealous or competitive. How could you have turned that feeling into support? How might that have changed your relationship?

✗ Challenge
This week, encourage a brother without expecting anything back. Notice his growth, celebrate his wins, and show you're on his side.

● Code to Remember
I will support my brothers' successes, knowing their journey doesn't threaten mine—it makes us stronger together.

PART V

Hearts & Honour: Lessons in Love

This part isn't about dating advice or cheesy pickup lines. It's about learning to lead with honour, respect yourself, and recognise what truly matters in a connection.

Love, attraction, and heartbreak will all come your way—but it's how you respond to them that defines you. You're not just figuring out relationships; you're figuring out who you are.

Because the way you love—and the way you recover—will shape more than just your heart. It'll shape your character.

1

Understanding Attraction—What Draws You In

◇◇◇◇◇

'Attraction isn't just about who catches your eye—it's about who keeps your mind and earns your respect.'

◇◇◇◇◇

Attraction isn't just about looks or charm. It's easy to get caught up in appearances, especially when you're younger—but real attraction goes deeper than that. As you grow, you'll start to notice that what truly draws you to someone often has more to do with how they think, how they carry themselves, and how they treat others than with anything on the surface.

The first thing to realise is that attraction isn't only about the other person—it's also about you. The way you speak, what you believe in, how you treat people, and how you carry yourself all shape the kind of people who are drawn to you. If you want a relationship that means something, you've got to bring something real to the table. That doesn't mean pretending to be perfect. It means being honest, kind, respectful, and confident in who you are becoming.

Pay close attention to how someone makes you feel—not just when things are exciting, but when things are calm or difficult. Do they show you respect, or do they test your boundaries? Do you feel more like yourself around them, or do you feel like you're trying too hard to impress? Someone might be attractive on the outside, but if being around them leaves you drained, anxious, or unsure, that's not something to ignore.

True attraction often reflects the things you care about most. If you value things like honesty, loyalty, and depth, you'll start to be more drawn to those qualities in others. And when you're clear on your values, you're far less likely to chase something that only looks good from a distance.

In the end, attraction isn't just a random feeling—it's a mirror. It shows you what you admire, what excites you, and even what kind of person you want to be. The more you understand it, the better your choices will be. And the better your choices, the stronger and more meaningful your connections will become.

◇◇◇◇◇

Reflection
What qualities do you find most attractive in others? Are they based on looks, personality, or shared values?

Something to Write About
Write down a few things that draw you to someone—whether it's a person you're currently attracted to or someone from your past. What stands out to you about those traits?

Challenge
Take note of the qualities you admire in others, and focus on developing those traits in yourself. It's not about changing who you are—but becoming someone who attracts what's real.

Code to Remember
I will focus on what truly attracts me to others and ensure I attract those who share my values and goals.

2

Who You're Drawn to Reveals What You Value

◇◇◇◇

'The kind of person you're drawn to is often a mirror of where you are in your own journey.'

◇◇◇◇

The qualities you're drawn to in a girl say more about you than they do about her. Are you looking for someone who challenges you to grow, or someone who simply gives you attention? Are you drawn to strength of character, or only to surface-level looks and status? Do you admire her values and mindset, or are you chasing a feeling to cover up insecurity?

When you're unsure of who you are, it's easy to be pulled toward comfort, attention, or validation. You might look for someone who fills a void rather than someone who reflects your standards. But when you're grounded—when you know your worth—you'll want someone who aligns with your mission, not just your moods. The kind of girl you pursue reveals how much you respect yourself. And if you're not proud of that reflection, it's a signal to level up—not settle down.

Back in *Part III, Day 6*, we talked about how your circle shapes your character. That includes the girl you choose to be close to. A girlfriend isn't just someone you spend time with—she can influence your thoughts, your habits, even your identity. And that influence can either sharpen your edge or dull it over time. If the relationship isn't helping you grow, what is it helping you do? Drift? Stall? Downplay yourself?

A real relationship isn't just about connection—it's about direction.

Looks can change, and will eventually fade. Popularity shifts. But integrity, loyalty, discipline, and purpose don't go out of style. If you want something that lasts, start by becoming a man who lives with clarity and strength. Then choose someone whose life points in the same direction. Someone who supports your purpose—not someone who becomes an escape from it.

A relationship should be an alliance, not a distraction. And becoming that kind of man starts with raising your own standards.

◇◇◇◇◇

Reflection
Think about the last time you found yourself attracted to someone. Was it based more on how they looked, how they made you feel, or who they were at their core?

Something to Write About
List three qualities you'd want in a future girlfriend that have nothing to do with looks or popularity. Now list three qualities you know *you* need to develop to attract someone like that.

Challenge
Observe how the girls around you treat others—friends, teachers, family, even strangers. Look beyond appearances and ask yourself: would I still respect her if she wasn't attractive to me?

Code to Remember
I will pursue someone who strengthens my future—not someone who distracts me from it.

3

Emotions Are Not Weaknesses—They're a Part of You

◇◇◇◇◇

'A man who can't face his own feelings will never have full control of his life.'

◇◇◇◇◇

It's easy to think emotions are something to hide. Society often tells boys and men to keep a straight face, to 'man up,' and to act like nothing bothers them. But let's set the record straight—emotions don't make you weak. They make you human.

Feeling something deeply means you care. It means you're alive. And recognising what you feel—instead of stuffing it down—is one of the strongest things you can do. Every emotion is like a message. Anger can show you that something's not fair. Sadness can reveal what matters most to you. Joy can remind you of what brings you life. These signals exist for a reason.

Ignoring your emotions doesn't make you tougher. It just makes it harder to understand what's really going on inside. Real strength isn't about being numb. It's about having the courage to face your feelings and the wisdom to respond instead of explode. You don't have to act on every emotion, but you should understand where they come from and decide how to handle them.

When you can name what you're feeling—like anger, guilt, fear, or stress—you give yourself a chance to handle it calmly and clearly. You're not being tossed around by your emotions. You're steering them. That's not weakness. That's control. That's leadership—not over others, but over yourself.

That's emotional maturity. It's knowing what's happening inside of you, being honest about it, and choosing how to move forward with a steady hand. You're not less of a man for feeling confused, hurt, frustrated, or afraid. You become more of one when you carry those emotions with honesty—without losing your head or your character.

Let what you feel guide you—but don't let it take the lead. Stay grounded. Stay focused. Let your emotions inform your decisions, not control them. They're part of your armour, not something to hide.

The more you understand your emotions, the more control you'll have over your reactions. That's how real men move—not by pretending they feel nothing, but by learning how to feel everything... without falling apart.

◇◇◇◇◇

▰ Reflection
What emotion do you tend to avoid or suppress the most? Why do you think that is?

▰ Something to Write About
Write about a recent time you felt something deeply—whether it was frustration, sadness, excitement, or fear. What do you think that emotion was trying to tell you?

✘ Challenge
Next time you feel overwhelmed, pause instead of reacting. Try to name the emotion. Then ask yourself what it might be pointing to.

● Code to Remember
I will not fear my feelings. I will face them, name them, and use them to grow stronger.

4

Setting Boundaries in Relationships

⬦⬦⬦⬦

'If you don't set the standard, someone else will set it for you—and it won't be in your favour.'

⬦⬦⬦⬦

Knowing your worth isn't enough—you have to protect it. That's where boundaries come in. They're not just rules or walls—they're clear lines that guard your time, energy, values, and peace of mind. Without them, people may test your limits, whether they mean to or not. And over time, that can slowly wear down your confidence and sense of self.

In every kind of relationship—friendship, family, dating—boundaries show strength, not selfishness. They're not about pushing people away. They're about making space for respect. When you set a boundary, you're not being rude. You're showing that you take yourself seriously. You know what you stand for. You know what's okay—and what's not.

Sometimes setting a boundary looks like saying 'no' to something that feels off. Other times, it means asking for space to think or breathe. It might mean calling out someone who crosses a line or choosing to step back when someone can't respect your limits. These actions take courage. But they also build self-respect.

Start simple. Think about your physical space—do people touch or crowd you in ways that make you uncomfortable? Your time—are others constantly pulling you away from your priorities? Your emotions—do you feel safe sharing how you feel, or are your feelings constantly dismissed? Your values—do you feel pressure to go against what you believe?

Boundaries are there to protect what matters to you. The people who care about you will respect them—and grow stronger with you because of them. The ones who don't? That's your signal. You're not responsible for managing their discomfort. You're responsible for standing firm in who you are.

You teach others how to treat you by what you allow. If you let people walk all over your lines, they'll keep doing it. But if you hold steady, you'll attract people who respect you for it. That's how solid relationships are built—with honesty, clarity, and a strong sense of self.

◇◇◇◇◇

▰ Reflection
Where in your life do you feel like your boundaries are being tested or ignored?

▰ Something to Write About
Write about a time you stayed silent when someone crossed a line. What could you have done differently—and what would you do next time?

✘ Challenge
Pick one boundary you've been avoiding and enforce it this week. Whether it's saying no, asking for space, or having a hard conversation—back yourself.

◉ Code to Remember
I will protect my time, space, and energy by setting clear boundaries and standing by them.

5

Lead with Honour, Not Ego

◇◇◇◇◇

'Ego wants to win. Honour wants to do what's right—even when it's not easy to do so.'

◇◇◇◇◇

In relationships, your character will always matter more than your charm. You might be able to impress someone at first with your confidence, looks, or the way you speak—but that only goes so far. Over time, what really counts is how you treat people, especially when no one's watching. That's what tells the true story of who you are.

A man led by ego seeks control, praise, and power. He wants to win, be admired, and have the final word. A man led by honour wants something deeper—mutual respect, truth, and real connection. He's not focused on being the loudest or the smartest. He's focused on being trustworthy and steady.

Ego turns every disagreement into a competition. Honour looks for understanding. Ego reacts to be seen. Honour responds to build peace. When ego leads, you might feel powerful in the moment, but that power fades fast. Ego creates distance. Honour creates respect.

Leading with honour doesn't mean letting people walk over you. It means standing firm without disrespecting others. It means being honest, even when it's uncomfortable. It means protecting someone's dignity, even when they've hurt you. That kind of strength doesn't shout—it stands tall and steady.

Honour shows up in how you apologise, how you listen, how you handle frustration. It's quiet, but powerful. The people who matter will notice. They'll feel safe with you. They'll know they can count on you—not just when it's easy, but especially when it's hard.

If you want to lead in a relationship, start with your character. Not with ego. Not with control. With honour. It's the foundation of strong love, lasting trust, and mutual growth. Ego may win followers for a moment, but honour earns loyalty that lasts.

Be the kind of man who leads from within. Who puts values above image. Who makes people feel respected, not small. Honour is the mark of a man worth following—and becoming.

◇◇◇◇◇

▦ Reflection
Have I ever let my ego lead me in a relationship or conversation? How did that turn out?

📔 Something to Write About
Describe the difference between acting with ego and acting with honour. Which one do you want to lead your future relationships?

⚔ Challenge
This week, catch yourself in a moment where your ego wants to win. Pause—and choose honour instead. It might be in a disagreement, a moment of jealousy, or a situation where you want to prove yourself.

➤ Code to Remember
I will lead with honour, even when it's harder than feeding my ego.

6

Talking to Girls Starts with Confidence

◇◇◇◇◇

'Confidence isn't about having all the answers. It's about being okay with who you are—even when you don't.'

◇◇◇◇◇

Talking to girls doesn't have to be complicated. What makes it feel overwhelming is fear—fear of being judged, fear of saying the wrong thing, or fear of looking like a complete idiot. That fear builds pressure, and pressure kills connection. But confidence? Confidence cuts through pressure every time.

Now, confidence doesn't mean being perfect. It means being secure in who you are. It's not about memorising clever lines or trying to act like someone you're not—it's about knowing your worth and showing up as your real self. Girls are drawn to authenticity. When you're honest, respectful, and fully present, that speaks louder than any smooth words ever could.

That said, presentation matters. If you want to carry yourself with confidence, it starts with how you show up. Clean, well-fitted clothes. Fresh breath, trimmed nails, washed face, neat hair, and so on. Good hygiene isn't about vanity—it's about self-respect. When you take care of yourself, it sends a message: 'I value who I am.'

Body language plays a role too. Stand tall. Shoulders back. Speak clearly. Don't mumble. Don't fidget. Make eye contact—not in a creepy way, but with respect and presence. A calm, grounded posture does more for your confidence than you might realise.

And don't forget the basics. Say hello. Be polite. Listen without interrupting. Ask questions that show you care about what the other person has to say. Confidence without manners quickly becomes arrogance—and nobody's impressed by arrogance.

Not every conversation will go somewhere—and that's fine. The goal isn't to 'win' every time. The goal is to practise being real, grounded, and socially aware. Every attempt is a step forward, even if it's awkward. Even if you stumble. The more you try, the easier it becomes.

Talking to girls starts with how you carry yourself. Be real. Be respectful. Be steady. That's confidence. And it's what makes all the difference.

◇◇◇◇◇

Reflection
What part of talking to someone new makes you most nervous—and how can you work on that?

Something to Write About
Describe how your appearance affects your confidence. What's one small change you could make that would boost it?

Challenge
Take extra care of your grooming this week, and start one conversation with someone new. Nothing forced—just show up well and be real.

Code to Remember
I will show up with confidence, take care of myself, and lead with respect in every conversation.

7

Why Respect Is More Important Than Validation

'Validation feeds the ego. Respect builds the man.'

There's a big difference between being liked and being respected. It's tempting to chase attention—compliments, approval, or the feeling of being noticed. Everyone wants to feel like they matter. But chasing validation is like drinking saltwater: it might feel refreshing at first, but it leaves you emptier in the end.

Validation is short-lived. It depends on moods, on whether others notice or praise you. Respect, on the other hand, lasts. It doesn't shift based on what's popular or what people expect. It's earned—through the way you carry yourself and the choices you make when no one's watching.

Validation is about how others see you.
Respect is about how you show up.

You don't get respect because you ask for it—or impress someone once. You earn it through consistency, honesty, and strong values. It's the result of building a reputation that's hard to shake, because it's real.

In friendships or relationships, it's easy to try to be liked. You might stay quiet, agree when you disagree, or change yourself to match who others want you to be. But when you chase validation, you're not being true—you're performing.

And if someone only likes you when you're easy to agree with, that's not real connection—it's convenience.

Respect begins with self-respect. It starts when you stop compromising just to keep the peace. When you speak up—not to be loud, but because your voice matters. When you take the harder path, not for praise, but because it's right.

The men people respect most don't need to be liked by everyone. They're grounded. They don't change direction every time the wind blows. They know who they are—and act like it.

If you're always chasing applause, you'll live by someone else's standards. But if you build your life around respect—especially self-respect—you'll attract people who value you for who you truly are.

And those are the people worth having in your corner.

◇◇◇◇◇

▥ Reflection:
Do you ever change who you are just to be liked? What would it look like to choose self-respect over approval?

▤ Something to Write About:
Describe a time when you chased validation instead of holding your ground. What did you learn from it?

✕ Challenge:
This week, when the urge for attention hits, pause. Choose what earns respect, even if it means standing alone.

◉ Code to Remember:
I will seek respect over attention, even when it's the harder path.

8

You're Not Ready for a Relationship If You Can't Be Alone

⬥⬥⬥⬥⬥

'Needing someone isn't the same as choosing someone—and love can't grow where fear lives.'

⬥⬥⬥⬥⬥

A relationship should be a choice, not a crutch. If the only reason you want to be with someone is because you can't stand being alone, then you're not ready for what a real relationship demands. Loneliness isn't cured by dating—it's cured by learning how to enjoy your own company.

Being alone doesn't mean you're broken or unwanted. It means you've got the space to figure out who you are without someone else shaping your identity. It's a time to build discipline, focus, and self-awareness. When you learn to be content on your own, you stop chasing people just to fill a gap. You start choosing people who truly align with you.

Being alone also helps you recognise what you want—and what you *don't* want. If you jump into a relationship just to avoid silence or stillness, you'll end up attaching to the wrong people for the wrong reasons. That's how you lose yourself. That's how you end up bending your values just to hold on to something that was never solid to begin with.

True strength shows up when you can sit in a room with nothing but your thoughts and not feel the need to escape. When you can stand on your own, you bring stability into a relationship. You don't expect someone else to fix you or make you feel complete. You've already done the work—and now you're ready to build something stronger, together.

So before you chase after a girlfriend, ask yourself: Can I be alone and still feel whole? Can I enjoy my own company? Can I build a life that already feels meaningful without waiting for someone else to give it meaning?

Learn to be your own anchor first. Know your values. Own your time. Face your thoughts. That's not just maturity—it's the foundation of every healthy connection you'll ever have. The stronger your roots, the more stable anything you grow with someone else will be.

◇◇◇◇◇

💬 Reflection:
Do you feel at peace when you're alone, or do you feel like something's missing?

📓 Something to Write About:
Describe a time when being alone taught you something important about yourself. What did it show you?

✘ Challenge:
Spend one full day without reaching for outside distractions or approval. Don't look for someone else to fill the silence or make you feel important. Just be with yourself. What do you notice when there's nothing to hide behind?

⦿ Code to Remember:
I will learn to stand strong on my own before I ask someone to stand beside me.

9

The Right Relationship Will Challenge You

◇◇◇◇◇

'The right person won't just make you feel good—they'll make you grow.'

◇◇◇◇◇

It's easy to think the perfect relationship should be smooth, easy, and full of constant affection. Effortless—like everything just clicks and nothing ever goes wrong. But that's not real life. The strongest relationships aren't built on comfort alone—they're built on challenge. The right person won't just admire you—they'll expect more from you. They'll call you out when you're off-track. They'll raise the bar to spark a fire in you—to push you toward the man you're meant to become. Not to control you, but to grow with you.

That kind of relationship isn't always easy. And it shouldn't be. Growth never is. A partner who truly cares about you won't just stroke your ego or avoid tough conversations. They'll speak up when they see you slipping. They'll tell you the truth when it matters. And they'll challenge you to keep becoming the man you say you want to be.

That doesn't mean the relationship becomes a battleground. It means there's space for accountability. A good partner doesn't shame you—they sharpen you. They challenge your excuses, not your worth. They want to see you win, but they're not afraid to call out what's holding you back.

Real compatibility isn't built on constant agreement. It's built on shared values, trust, and the ability to have hard conversations with honesty and respect. A relationship like that will test your pride. It'll stretch your patience. And if you're willing to stay present, it will shape your character.

So if someone challenges you—especially when it's uncomfortable—pause before you get defensive. Ask yourself where it's coming from. Are they criticising you to feel powerful, or are they calling you forward because they believe in you? The difference is massive.

A partner who pushes you to be better is rare. Don't mistake that for conflict. It's a sign of respect. It means they see your potential—and they're not content watching you settle for less than what you're capable of.

◇◇◇◇◇

💬 Reflection:
How do you respond when someone challenges you in a relationship? Do you shut down—or lean in?

📓 Something to Write About:
Write about a time someone held you accountable in a way that helped you grow. How did it feel, and what did it teach you?

⚔ Challenge:
Look at your closest relationships. Are they helping you grow, or keeping you comfortable? Choose one way to step up and show growth this week.

⊘ Code to Remember:
I will welcome the kind of challenges that help me grow into a better man.

10

Don't Lose Yourself to Please Someone Else

⬦⬦⬦⬦

'Real love will never ask or require you to sacrifice your identity. Respecting yourself is the first step in respecting others.'

⬦⬦⬦⬦

It's easy to fall into the trap of becoming who you think someone wants you to be—especially when you're chasing approval, attention, or love. You start shifting the way you talk, the way you dress, even the things you care about, hoping to earn their acceptance. But in doing so, you begin to drift. Slowly, quietly, you lose touch with your own values, your passions, and the parts of you that make you, you. That's not a relationship—it's self-abandonment disguised as love.

A strong relationship doesn't ask you to hold yourself back—it calls you to show up as your full, honest self. When you feel like you have to constantly perform or hide parts of who you are, that's not a healthy connection—it's a warning sign. Because pretending might win someone's attention for a while, but it can't earn their respect. And over time, it leads to resentment, confusion, and burnout.

Authenticity takes courage. It means standing firm in what matters to you—even if it means not being everyone's cup of tea. It means knowing your values, your boundaries, and your goals well enough to not trade them for short-term validation. You weren't meant to be a watered-down version of yourself just to keep someone around. You are worthy of love and respect for who you truly are, not for who you pretend to be.

When someone truly respects you, they'll want you to thrive as you are—not as a version crafted to make them comfortable. And if someone walks away because you were being real? Let them. That kind of honesty saves you from years of pretending.

Stay rooted in who you are. Relationships built on truth last longer, feel better, and lead to real growth. You don't have to lose yourself to be loved. The right connection won't require you to.

Be true. Be steady. And let the right people rise to meet you.

◇◇◇◇◇

💬 Reflection
Think about a time when you felt like you compromised too much of yourself in a relationship. How did it feel? What were the long-term effects on your self-esteem?

📓 Something to Write About
Write about what makes you unique. What are the qualities that define you? How can you make sure to hold onto those qualities, even in the face of pressure to change?

✂ Challenge
Over the next week, be aware of moments when you might be tempted to change yourself to please others. Challenge yourself to stay true to your values, even when it's difficult. Recognise that your worth is not defined by others' approval.

🏅 Code to Remember
Don't let anyone make you feel like you have to change who you are to be loved. The right people will love you for who you are.

11

Earned Respect Matters More Than Easy Attention

◇◇◇◇◇

'Anyone can get attention. The real challenge is earning respect.'

◇◇◇◇◇

It's easy to be loud. It's easy to do something flashy or attention-grabbing. But just because people are looking at you doesn't mean they respect you. Attention is cheap. Respect is earned.

Some will do anything to be noticed—brag, exaggerate, show off, even act out in ways that go against who they truly are. But those things fade. They're noise. Temporary. They don't leave a lasting impression where it truly counts. The kind of recognition that matters isn't handed out for being the centre of attention. It's given to those who consistently show up with character, who live in a way that others admire quietly, even when no one says it out loud.

Respect comes when people see that you're honest, reliable, and thoughtful. It builds slowly, through quiet strength and steady choices. You don't need to perform for it. You just need to live like it matters.

Respect has weight. It's earned in how you carry yourself when no one's watching, how you speak to those who can do nothing for you, and how you stand firm in your values—especially when it's inconvenient. That's when it really counts. That's when people notice.

You don't need a stage or applause to matter. The person who earns respect doesn't chase it—they draw it naturally by how they live. Their reputation is built not on moments, but on consistency. Their presence doesn't demand attention—it commands it, without ever needing to shout.

When you focus on living with integrity, the right people will take notice—not because you made the most noise, but because you stood for something when it was easier not to. The spotlight will always shift, but respect lasts. It's not about impressing others for a moment. It's about becoming the kind of man they can count on for a lifetime.

Earned respect is one of the strongest foundations you can build. And once you have it, it can open doors, build trust, and create bonds that shallow attention never could.

◇◇◇◇◇

Reflection
Who's someone you genuinely respect? What do they do that earns your admiration? How can you mirror that?

Something to Write About
List three ways you can earn more respect this week. What actions will show integrity and consistency?

Challenge
For the next seven days, focus on earning respect—be steady, kind, and true to your values. Watch how others respond.

Code to Remember
Attention fades quickly. Respect sticks around for the long run.

12

Knowing When to Walk Away

◇◇◇◇◇

'Sometimes, walking away isn't failure. It's strength, wisdom, and self-respect.'

◇◇◇◇◇

One of the hardest lessons to learn in life is knowing when to walk away. It can feel like quitting. Like you're giving up. But what's important to understand is: walking away isn't always a sign of weakness. In many cases, it's a clear sign of strength. It means you're choosing long-term peace over short-term comfort. It means you're setting a higher standard for yourself.

Some people stay in unhealthy relationships out of guilt, fear, or the belief that things might magically change. But if someone consistently disrespects your boundaries, belittles your values, or leaves you feeling drained more often than uplifted—it's time to ask the hard question: What am I actually holding onto?

You don't owe anyone your continued presence if they're causing more harm than good. Loyalty isn't about staying no matter what—it's about showing up for people who also show up for you. A real relationship, whether it's romantic, friendly, or even family, should help you grow. It should bring strength, not strip it away.

There's a difference between working through challenges and being stuck in a cycle that's hurting you. If something keeps costing you your peace, your confidence, or your sense of direction, you have every right to leave it behind.

Walking away doesn't mean you didn't care. It means you cared enough about your own future to stop settling for less than you deserve. Sometimes the most courageous thing you can do is to stop hoping someone will change—and start changing the direction of your own life instead.

Next time you feel torn between staying and going, ask yourself honestly: Is this helping me become better? Or is this breaking me down? Listen to your gut. Listen to your values. You're not weak for walking away. You're wise for recognising when enough is enough.

Your life is too valuable to waste on what drains you. Walk away with your head held high—and don't look back.

◇◇◇◇◇

▪ Reflection
Think of a time when you stayed in a situation longer than you should have. What made it hard to walk away? How did it impact your peace and self-worth?

▪ Something to Write About
Write about a time when you knew walking away was best but hesitated. What held you back? How could you have handled it differently?

✕ Challenge
Assess the relationships in your life. Are any draining you more than they empower you? If so, consider setting boundaries or walking away for the sake of your peace and growth.

● Code to Remember
Walking away is not a sign of weakness. It's a sign of strength, wisdom, and self-respect.

13

Rejection Isn't the End of You

◇◇◇◇◇

'Rejection isn't a verdict. It's just proof you were brave enough to try.'

◇◇◇◇◇

Rejection hurts—there's no way around it. Whether it's from someone you like, a group you want to belong to, or an opportunity that slips through your fingers, the sting is real. But i: rejection doesn't define you. It's how you respond to it that counts.

A lot of guys take rejection personally. They start to believe they're not good enough, not attractive enough, or simply not wanted. The thing is, most of the time, rejection isn't about you being 'less than.' It's about a mismatch. Maybe she wasn't ready. Maybe it wasn't the right fit. Or maybe life has something better lined up for you. That doesn't change your worth. You're not diminished by someone else's choices. Your value remains unchanged, no matter how the situation plays out.

The real danger of rejection isn't the sting itself—it's how you react to it. If you let rejection make you hold yourself back, you're hurting your future growth. If you stop putting yourself out there, stop trying, stop caring—then you've lost. Growth only happens when you're willing to risk. When you put yourself out there despite the uncertainty. When you step up, knowing that sometimes things won't go your way, but you keep moving forward anyway.

Remember, you don't need everyone to say yes. You just need to keep showing up as someone who refuses to quit when things get tough.

Rejection is not failure—it's feedback. It's a signal that there's room to learn, to grow, and to refine. The pain may not feel great, but it's part of the process. Every 'no' is an opportunity to adjust, to strengthen, and to keep going.

So the next time you face rejection, remind yourself of this: If you have the courage to face a 'no,' you've already shown more strength than most. Keep pushing forward. Stay in the game. Because the only way to truly fail is to stop trying.

Never let rejection stop you from reaching the next level, and don't forget that each setback brings you closer to a breakthrough. In the end, rejection is just another stepping stone on your path to success.

◇◇◇◇◇

💬 Reflection
How do you usually respond to rejection? What thoughts come up?

📓 Something to Write About
Write about a time you were rejected. What did you learn from it that helped you grow?

⚔ Challenge
Think about something you've been avoiding because you're afraid of rejection. Take one small, safe step toward it this week—just enough to prove to yourself that rejection won't break you.

🧭 Code to Remember
I will face rejection without losing confidence in who I am.

14

You Teach People How to Treat You

⋄⋄⋄⋄⋄

'The way you allow others to treat you is a direct reflection of how you treat yourself.'

⋄⋄⋄⋄⋄

How people treat you speaks volumes about who they are. But what really reveals your character is how you allow others to treat you. Your self-respect is reflected in the way you set boundaries, uphold standards, and present yourself to the world. If you allow disrespect or tolerate behaviour that doesn't align with your values, you're sending a message that it's okay. Over time, others will take advantage of that, and you may find yourself in situations where you're constantly overlooked or undervalued.

On the flip side, when you demand respect and set a standard for how you expect to be treated, you teach others to do the same. This isn't about being rigid or unyielding; it's about understanding your worth and acting accordingly. The respect you have for yourself becomes the blueprint for how others will treat you. You don't need to shout it from the rooftops—you show it through your actions, words, and decisions. You teach people how to treat you by how you treat yourself.

Self-respect isn't about being arrogant, expecting perfection, or thinking that everyone should cater to your every whim. It's about recognising your value and ensuring that your actions and behaviour reflect that understanding. When you value yourself, you attract people who will appreciate that value too. But when you lower your standards to avoid conflict, to seek approval, or to fit in, you're telling people that disrespect is acceptable. And that creates a pattern that's difficult to break.

Setting boundaries is a vital part of this. Boundaries aren't just about saying 'no' when something doesn't feel right. They're about teaching people where the line is and holding them accountable when they cross it. If you fail to set clear boundaries, others will impose their own limits on you—and those limits may not respect your worth.

In the end, you are the standard. The better you treat yourself, the better others will treat you. You set the tone for how people treat you, and that tone starts with you. So, hold yourself to the standard of respect you deserve.

◇◇◇◇◇

Reflection
Are people in your life treating you with the respect you deserve? Are you being treated with respect? Where have you let things slide to avoid conflict? What needs to change?

Something to Write About
List how you let others treat you. Where have you lowered your standards? Then write what respectful treatment looks like—and what changes you need to make.

Challenge
Choose one area where you've allowed disrespect. Set a boundary today—and stick to it.

Code to Remember
Respect starts with me, and I'll never let anyone treat me less than I deserve.

PART VI

Courage, Challenge & Purpose

Courage isn't about feeling fearless—it's about showing up anyway. Every challenge you face is a chance to grow stronger, and every fear you confront brings you closer to the man you're meant to become.

This part will push you to lean into discomfort, face failure with grit, and stop waiting for purpose to find you. You'll learn to create it.

This is where your edge gets sharpened. No shortcuts—just the road every real man must walk.

1

The World Won't Hand You Purpose—You Create It

◇◇◇◇◇

'Purpose isn't something you wait to find—it's something you forge, step by step, through action, effort, and meaning.'

◇◇◇◇◇

Purpose isn't something that drops into your life out of nowhere. It won't appear while you're waiting around, hoping for clarity or inspiration to strike. The world isn't going to hand it to you on a silver plate, and no one else can define it for you. It's something you create—through your choices, your consistency, and your willingness to face the challenges that shape you.

Purpose is built slowly, over time. It's the result of showing up, day after day, and choosing to push through even when it's hard. It starts to take shape when you take ownership of your life—when you stop drifting and start driving. When you stop blaming and start building. Purpose doesn't thrive in comfort. It's forged in discomfort, in adversity, in the quiet battles no one else sees.

A lot of guys look for purpose in titles, relationships, money, or recognition. But none of those things can give you lasting meaning. Real purpose comes from within—from what you value, what you believe in, and what you're willing to stand for when it counts. It's not about chasing something impressive. It's about becoming someone solid.

Every day gives you a chance to live with intention. The way you show up—how you handle pressure, how you treat others, how you carry yourself—either builds or weakens your sense of purpose. It's not about finding the perfect path. It's about choosing a direction that matters and walking it with conviction, even when it's tough.

And here's the key: purpose isn't just about what you do. It's about why you do it. It's knowing what drives you. It's getting up in the morning with a reason to push forward—not just because you have to, but because it matters to you. Purpose isn't a one-time decision. It's a way of living. It's the path you choose to walk—step by step, day by day.

No one's going to hand it to you. But you can build it—if you're willing to earn it.

◇◇◇◇◇

Reflection:
What is something you've always felt drawn to, but never committed to fully? Why do you think that is?

Something to Write About:
Write down one area of your life where you can begin taking ownership and actively pursue a greater purpose. What steps can you take this week to make it happen?

Challenge:
Take the first step toward your purpose today, no matter how small. Even if it's just deciding on one thing you'll start to commit to, take action.

Code to Remember:
I create my purpose through my actions.

2

Fear Isn't the Enemy. Avoidance Is.

⋄⋄⋄⋄⋄

'Fear is a signal—not a stop sign. What you avoid today will control you tomorrow.'

⋄⋄⋄⋄⋄

Fear is part of every man's life—it comes with being human. But fear itself isn't the problem. It's how you respond to it that defines your strength. The real enemy isn't fear; it's avoidance.

When you avoid what scares you, you shrink your world. You train yourself to retreat, to hide, and to choose comfort over courage. Over time, this avoidance erodes your confidence, weakens your direction, and damages your belief in your own abilities. The more you run from fear, the more power you give it—and the less trust you place in yourself to handle hard things.

Courage isn't the absence of fear—it's the decision to act in spite of it. Fear might whisper in your ear, trying to make you freeze—but you don't have to let it call the shots. Courage is choosing to move forward even when your heart is pounding and your mind is shouting at you to pull back.

When you lean into what you'd rather avoid, you start taking back control. Each uncomfortable, imperfect step forward builds strength—and teaches you to carry fear with you, not be stopped by it. You prove that fear doesn't make your decisions—you do.

Here's the reality: anything truly worthwhile will come with fear.

Starting something new. Speaking your mind in a hard conversation. Setting boundaries with people who push too far. Chasing a vision that no one else understands. These things require guts—not fearlessness, but the ability to act while still feeling afraid.

Fear isn't weakness—it's a signal that something matters. It means you're pushing your limits, stepping into new territory, and growing into a stronger version of yourself. The next time fear shows up—and it will—don't treat it like a wall. Treat it like a door. Step through it. On the other side is growth, self-respect, and the proof that you're becoming the man you were meant to be.

This is how courage is built—one bold, uncomfortable choice at a time. Don't back off. Lean into it. That's where true strength is forged—and where real change begins.

◇◇◇◇◇

💬 Reflection
What's something you've been avoiding lately out of fear? How has that avoidance impacted you?

📓 Something to Write About
Write about a time you faced fear head-on. What did it teach you?

✘ Challenge
Do one thing this week that you've been putting off because it scares you. It doesn't need to be perfect—just get it done.

❷ Code to Remember
I will face fear with action, not avoidance.

3

Every Setback Is a Step If You Stand Back Up

◇◇◇◇◇

'Failure isn't the end—it's feedback. You'll fall, but you'll learn from it. But no matter what happens, don't ever quit.'

◇◇◇◇◇

Every man fails. You will mess up. You'll try your hardest, and sometimes it still won't be enough. You might fall short despite giving it everything you've got. That doesn't make you weak—it makes you human. Failure is part of the journey. The real danger isn't in failing. It's in quitting.

Failure is a teacher, but only if you're willing to learn from it. It shows you where to improve, what you need to change, and what you're made of when everything falls apart. But to truly learn, you have to stay in the game. If you run from failure or let it define who you are, you lose out on the valuable lessons it could've given you. The hardest lessons are often the most important.

Some men fear failure so much that they never even try. They let the fear of falling short keep them stuck. Others take one hit and give up just before the breakthrough. They don't realise that growth is earned in those difficult moments—when things aren't going your way, but you keep pushing forward anyway. The men who make real progress aren't the ones who never fail, but the ones who refuse to quit when the going gets tough. It's those who show up again and again, learning from their mistakes, adjusting, and getting better. They develop resilience with every setback.

Why does this matter? Because life will test you. Challenges will come at you from every direction. But the men who rise up and grow into something real—into leaders, protectors, builders—are the ones who don't quit when failure knocks them down. They get back up and keep moving forward, learning how to handle even tougher challenges.

You don't need to be perfect. You don't need to have it all figured out. You just need to be persistent. Every time you fall and stand back up, you're building something unshakeable. That's where true confidence comes from—not from some illusion of perfection, but from earned resilience and the lessons learnt in the trenches.

So, fail forward. Learn hard. Stand back up. That's how strong men are made.

◇◇◇◇◇

▣ Reflection
What's one failure that taught you something important? How did it help you grow?

▤ Something to Write About
Describe a time you almost gave up. What kept you going? What did you learn from pushing through?

✕ Challenge
Pick one area in your life where fear of failure has been holding you back. Take one bold action toward it this week.

❷ Code to Remember
I will fail forward—but I will not quit.

4

Run Toward the Fire—The Forge Is Never Comfortable

◇◇◇◇

'When challenge calls, I won't run—I'll rise. That's how I'll become who I'm meant to be.'

◇◇◇◇

Most people run from discomfort. They avoid tension, challenge, pressure—anything that feels too heavy, too uncertain, or too raw. But every time you turn away, you miss a chance to grow. Real strength isn't built in safety. It's forged in the fire—when life gets unpredictable, when the pressure rises, when you don't know if you've got what it takes... but you show up anyway.

Running toward the fire doesn't mean being reckless or charging into chaos without a plan. It means choosing courage when hiding would be easier. It means doing the difficult thing on purpose. You stop making excuses. You stop playing small. You step forward while your heart is still pounding.

Growth lives in the heat. That's where your edges are tested. Where discipline is deepened. Where resilience is born. The fire exposes your weaknesses—but it also tempers your strengths. And if you keep showing up, day after day, the flames won't consume you. They'll shape you into something harder to break, harder to rattle, and harder to knock off course.

This is how men are made: not through ease, but through challenge. Not by avoiding hardship, but by walking straight into it. Discomfort isn't your enemy—it's your proving ground. When you lean into the flames—into the tough conversation, the higher standard, the hard decision—you separate yourself from the pack. You become someone who doesn't flinch when it counts.

Fire doesn't just burn. It reveals. It purifies. It leaves only what's solid—what's real. And the more you face it, the more control you gain over your fear, your temper, your impulses. You stop being reactive and start becoming refined.

The forge was never meant to be comfortable. It was meant to shape iron into steel. It was meant to burn away what's soft so that what remains can carry weight.

So run toward the fire—not to suffer, but to strengthen. Because that's where your edge is. That's where you become a man you can trust.

◇◇◇◇◇

🗩 Reflection
What's one challenge you've been avoiding? Why?

📓 Something to Write About
What would it look like to 'run toward the fire' in your life this week?

⚔ Challenge
Pick one uncomfortable action you've been resisting—and do it within the next twenty-four hours.

❂ Code to Remember
I will run toward the fire, because that's where I grow.

5

You Don't Need All the Answers— Ask Better Questions

◇◇◇◇

'The right question will unlock a world of possibility. Don't wait for all the answers—seek the truth.'

◇◇◇◇

A lot of men waste time trying to find the perfect answer before taking action. They stall. They overthink. They convince themselves that one more insight, one more sign, one more certainty will finally unlock the right move. But life doesn't work that way. It doesn't pause until you're ready. The answers won't always come at once, and you'll never know everything you need to know to make a perfect decision.

What matters isn't having all the answers—it's learning to ask the right questions. Good questions lead to better thinking, clearer direction, and more effective action. They force you to dig deeper, challenge assumptions, and see things from a new angle. It's not about knowing it all; it's about knowing how to look for what matters.

Start there, and ask yourself:
- What's really holding me back?
- What am I pretending not to know?
- What does this situation require from me—not just what do I want to gain from it?

The better the questions you ask, the better your clarity becomes. And with clarity, comes action.

Asking the right questions shifts your mindset. Instead of getting stuck in doubt or fear, you move toward growth. You stop playing defence and start thinking like a builder. A strategist. A man who's looking for an opening, not an excuse. When you feel lost, don't freeze up—go deeper. Ask: 'What's the lesson here?' 'What can I control right now?' 'How can I turn this into something that makes me stronger?'

It's through these questions that you grow. They're your compass in the fog. Your way forward when the path isn't obvious. You don't need to have all the answers figured out—you just need to stay in the fight long enough to find them. That's what separates the men who drift from the men who lead.

In the end, the man who keeps asking better questions never stays stuck for long. He sharpens his thinking. He takes ownership. And eventually—he finds the answers worth living by.

◇◇◇◇◇

▣ Reflection
Think of a situation where you felt stuck. What question could've helped you see it differently?

📓 Something to Write About
What's one area of your life where asking better questions could lead to growth?

✘ Challenge
This week, when you face a challenge, replace 'Why is this happening to me?' with 'What can I learn from this?'

◉ Code to Remember
I will ask better questions and let them shape the man I become.

6

Pain Is a Message—Listen, Learn, Then Push Through

⋄⋄⋄⋄

'Pain isn't your enemy. It's the signal that something important is happening. Pay attention, then keep moving.'

⋄⋄⋄⋄

Pain is something every man encounters. Whether physical, emotional, or mental, it's inevitable. But pain isn't something to shy away from. It's a message—one that too many ignore. Your body, mind, or spirit is telling you that you're being stretched beyond what's comfortable. And that's exactly where growth begins.

Whether it's the sting of failure, the burn from a brutal workout, the ache of rejection, or the heartbreak of personal loss—pain holds valuable insight. It's not just there to hurt you. It's there to teach you. When you face pain, don't just survive it—study it. Reflect: What can I take from this? What does it reveal about my limits, my choices, or my expectations?

Pain shows you where you're weak—but it also highlights where you're capable of becoming strong. It uncovers the gaps. The more you lean into those lessons, the more solid you become. Men who grow aren't those who avoid pain—they're the ones who face it head-on, learn what they need to, and keep going anyway.

Choosing to push through pain doesn't mean ignoring it. It means listening closely, taking note of what matters, and refusing to let it control you. That's how character is built. With every setback that doesn't break you, you build resolve. With every tear or trial that doesn't make you quit, you gain grit.

Eventually, you'll start to see pain differently. It won't feel like an enemy. It'll feel like a familiar teacher—tough, direct, but invested in your progress. When you can walk through pain with your head high and your eyes open, you stop being at its mercy. You become something stronger than it.

Pain isn't an obstacle. It's part of the journey. Proof that you're moving forward, evolving, and sharpening into a man who's dangerous to weakness, failure, and fear itself.

Listen to it. Learn from it. Then push through it.

Because that's how men are made.

◇◇◇◇◇

💬 Reflection
Think about a painful experience you've faced. What lesson did it offer you?

📓 Something to Write About
What's one area of your life where you could view pain as a signal for growth?

✖ Challenge
Identify a current challenge. Instead of avoiding it, lean into it and see what you can learn from the discomfort.

🧭 Code to Remember
I will embrace pain as a message, because that's where I'll grow stronger.

7

Forge Yourself Through Challenge

◇◇◇◇◇

'If you only do what's easy, you'll stay the same. You grow by doing what you'd rather avoid.'

◇◇◇◇◇

There's a difference between reacting to pain and choosing discomfort. One is survival. The other is strength. Most people only face difficulty when they have no choice—when life forces it on them. But if you want to grow into a man of purpose, confidence, and control, you can't wait for life to rough you up. You've got to walk into the hard things willingly. On your own terms.

Discomfort isn't always punishment. Sometimes, it's preparation. Cold showers. Brutal workouts. Early mornings. Difficult conversations. Standing your ground. Speaking hard truths. These aren't just tests—they're tools. Tools that train your mind to obey you, not your emotions. Tools that remind your body who's in charge. Every time you step into discomfort with purpose, you prove something powerful: that your fear, your laziness, your doubts—they don't get the final say.

The men who grow are the ones who lean into resistance. They understand that discipline isn't born from ease—it's forged through friction. Most people look for the smooth road. But if you want to separate yourself, do what most won't. Choose the harder path. Repeatedly. Consistently. Not because it's glamorous. But because it works—and it lasts.

This isn't about chasing pain for the sake of suffering. It's about doing what needs to be done, even when you'd rather not. That's where grit is built. That's where character is shaped. Every hard thing you tackle—by choice—adds another layer to your foundation. You're stacking proof that you don't need comfort to stay committed, and that your strength isn't dependent on convenience.

You're not here to play it safe. You're not here to avoid struggle. You're here to become something better. That takes pressure. It takes heat. It takes friction. And it takes relentless, voluntary effort that sharpens you over time.

You're not after perfection. You're after progress.

And when you train in discomfort, you're not just building a body or a mindset.

You're building a legacy.

◇◇◇◇◇

💬 Reflection
What's one hard thing you've been avoiding that you know would make you stronger?

📕 Something to Write About
Write about a time when you chose the harder path. What did it teach you?

⚔ Challenge
This week, do one thing each day that makes you uncomfortable—on purpose.

🧭 Code to Remember
I will seek out challenge because comfort won't make me stronger.

8

Bravery Begins with Action

◇◇◇◇

'Courage doesn't mean you're not scared. It means you keep going even when you are.'

◇◇◇◇

Fear is something everyone experiences, no matter who you are. Whether it's the first day at a new school, speaking in front of a crowd, or trying something unfamiliar, fear is always there. But what separates the guys who grow from the ones who stay stuck is how they respond to that fear. Do they back down—or do they keep going?

It's easy to let fear take control. It can convince you to stay comfortable, to play it safe, and to avoid anything that feels risky. But growth doesn't happen in the safe zone. It happens when you step into the unknown—when you lean into the fear instead of running from it. That's the place where you start to level up.

Courage isn't about having zero fear. It's about moving forward *with* fear sitting in the passenger seat. It's showing up, taking action, and doing what needs to be done—even if your voice shakes or your hands tremble. Most people wait for fear to disappear before they try. But fear doesn't vanish. You just get stronger.

The secret? You build confidence by doing the thing *while* you're scared. Every time you face something uncomfortable and take that first step, you prove to yourself that fear isn't in charge. And the more you do that, the more trust you build in your own ability to handle what's next.

Think of it like training. The first few reps are shaky, but the more you show up, the more steady you get. Courage is built the same way—through reps. The more you do the hard things, the more you realise you're stronger than your fear.

So, stop waiting to feel brave. Stop waiting for the fear to go away. Go do the thing—even scared. That's where courage begins. That's where growth kicks in. And that's where you start becoming the kind of man who doesn't back down when it counts.

◇◇◇◇◇

💬 Reflection
Think about a time when you were scared to do something, but you did it anyway. How did it feel after you took action? What did you learn about yourself?

📓 Something to Write About
What's something right now that scares you? What's holding you back from facing it? What's the worst that could happen if you went for it?

✘ Challenge
This week, choose something you're afraid of and do it. It doesn't have to be big, but it has to be something that pushes you outside your comfort zone. Reflect on how you feel before, during, and after.

⊘ Code to Remember
I will choose action, even when I'm scared, because that's how I get stronger.

9

Courage Isn't Loud—It's Consistent

◇◇◇◇◇

'Courage isn't about being the loudest. It's about showing up, doing what needs to be done, and keeping your word—no matter what.'

◇◇◇◇◇

Courage isn't about big moves or making a scene. It's about consistency. It's about doing the right thing, even when it's tough, boring, or thankless. The real measure of courage is found in the quiet moments—the ones no one else sees. When it's just you, your thoughts, and the decision in front of you. That's where courage is forged.

It's easy to talk a big game. To repeat clever quotes, give advice, or tell others what you'll do. But words are cheap. Strength isn't in what's said—it's in what's done. What matters is whether you show up when it counts. Whether you keep showing up and stay the course when life tries to knock you down. That's where strength is built—not in the noise, but in the discipline. Discipline doesn't make noise, but it absolutely leaves a mark.

When you consistently choose to do what's difficult—when you honour your commitments, push through discomfort, and do what's right even when it's not rewarded—you're building something far more powerful than a single bold act. You're building a life of integrity. And integrity is the backbone of real courage.

Courage isn't a one-time event. It's not a speech, a stunt, or a moment of glory. It's a habit. It lives in the early mornings when you train while others sleep. It lives in the decisions to stay focused when distractions tempt you to quit. It lives in how you treat people when there's nothing to gain from it.

And yes, there will be days when it feels like no one sees your efforts. Like your consistency isn't appreciated or your strength goes unnoticed. But here's the thing: the men who make the biggest difference aren't always the loudest. They're the ones who show up. Every day. Without applause. Without shortcuts.

Real courage doesn't always look like a hero charging into battle. Sometimes, it's getting up when you're tired. Staying the course when it would be easier to quit. Choosing principle over comfort. Choosing responsibility over ease.

Courage is being steady. Reliable. Grounded. Not just when it's easy—but especially when it's not. If you can keep walking that path, day in and day out, you won't just be brave. You'll be someone others can count on. And that's rare.

◇◇◇◇◇

💬 Reflection
Think of a time when you showed courage in a quiet way. What did that look like, and how did it make you feel?

📓 Something to Write About
Where in your life can you show more consistent courage? What's one small action you can take today?

✘ Challenge
Identify one area of your life where you need to be more consistent. Take one small action today to show up and follow through.

⊙ Code to Remember
I will be consistent in my courage, doing what needs to be done, even when it's tough.

10

Don't Wait to Feel Ready

◇◇◇◇◇

'You'll never feel completely ready. Take the leap, and trust that you'll figure it out as you go.'

◇◇◇◇◇

A lot of guys wait for the perfect moment to act. They wait until they feel ready—until they have everything figured out, until the timing is right, until fear disappears completely. But the problem with this is, that moment may never come. Life doesn't wait for you to feel ready. As a matter of fact, it never does. It throws you into situations that demand action, usually before you're ever fully prepared for it. And that's okay. Because readiness isn't a feeling—it's a decision.

Waiting until you feel ready to do something means you're delaying your own growth. The thing is, you'll never be completely prepared for the real challenges that shape you. There will always be questions you can't answer yet, risks you can't fully control, and gaps in what you know. But those aren't reasons to hold back. They're invitations to step forward and grow into the man the challenge needs you to be.

Growth doesn't happen by standing still. It happens when you move, when you take the first step without knowing exactly where it'll lead. It happens when you stop obsessing over doing it perfectly and start showing up, learning, and adapting as you go. Action builds clarity. Momentum builds confidence.

Instead of waiting for the perfect conditions, choose to act anyway. Say yes to the opportunity. Start the project. Speak up. Take responsibility.

You don't need to have all the answers—you just need the courage to begin. You'll figure it out one step at a time. And along the way, you'll learn what you're really made of.

It's normal to feel uncertain. It's normal to feel nervous. But the men who grow into leaders, builders, and protectors aren't the ones who waited until they felt fearless—they're the ones who moved forward in spite of their fear.

So don't wait to feel ready. Choose to be ready. Choose to step into the unknown. That decision is what separates the man who watches life happen from the one who shapes it.

◇◇◇◇◇

💬 Reflection
What's something you've been putting off because you didn't feel ready? What would happen if you took the first step, even without feeling prepared?

📓 Something to Write About
Think of an area in your life where you've waited to feel ready. What's one small action you can take to start moving forward today?

✘ Challenge
Take one step today in an area where you've been waiting to feel ready. Even if it's uncomfortable, trust that the action will help you grow.

⊘ Code to Remember
I will take the leap, even if I don't feel ready, because that's when I'll learn and grow.

11

You're Stronger Than You Think

◇◇◇◇◇

'Strength isn't just about how much you can lift—it's about how much you can handle when life pushes back.'

◇◇◇◇◇

It's easy to doubt yourself when life gets hard. You start to question whether you've got what it takes, whether you're strong enough to carry the weight you're under. But strength isn't a trait some men are born with and others aren't—it's built. It's forged in the heat of challenge, pressure, and persistence. Every time you push through something difficult, whether or not anyone sees it, you're growing stronger in ways you might not even realise yet.

You've already proven that. Look back. There have been moments where you wanted to give up—times you were exhausted, overwhelmed, or hurting—but you didn't quit. You kept going. Maybe it wasn't perfect. Maybe it wasn't fast. But you moved forward anyway. That matters more than you realise. Because strength isn't about ease—it's about endurance. It's about showing up even when everything in you wants to walk away and quitting seems like the easier choice.

You've handled more than you give yourself credit for. Hard conversations. Personal losses. Mental battles that no one else saw. The challenges you've already survived are proof of what you're capable of. Every setback you've faced and risen from has added to the quiet foundation of your strength, even in ways you haven't yet seen. You've proven that you can handle adversity with grace, and that resilience is key.

And here's what happens when you stop underestimating yourself: you begin to face obstacles differently. They stop looking like dead ends and start looking like tests. Not of your worth—but of your will. When you stop running from difficulty and start leaning into it, you discover that your strength goes deeper than you thought, into parts of you that have yet to be fully tapped.

You don't need to have all the answers. You don't need to be the best, the fastest, or the strongest man in the room. You just need to keep going. That's the kind of strength that builds leaders, earns respect, and shapes the man you're becoming.

So the next time you doubt yourself—pause. Take a breath. And remember: you've made it through worse. You've grown through trials. You've carried weight that would've broken a lesser man. You're stronger than you think. And you're not done yet.

◇◇◇◇◇

▰ Reflection
Think about a moment when you thought you couldn't keep going, but you did. What did that teach you about your strength?

▰ Something to Write About
What's an area of your life where you can remind yourself of your strength and push through the next challenge?

✘ Challenge
Pick a challenge you're facing and break it into smaller steps. Take one action today, even if it's small.

❷ Code to Remember
I will face challenges with the confidence that I am stronger than I think, because every step forward builds my strength.

12

Step Into Your Calling

◇◇◇◇◇

'Your purpose isn't something you find—it's something you step into, one choice at a time.'

◇◇◇◇◇

Many people spend their lives searching for their purpose, as if it's a destination they can reach or a hidden treasure they'll stumble across. But purpose isn't found; it's created. It's not waiting for you somewhere out there—it's built through how you live, how you lead, and how you choose to show up every single day.

Purpose is shaped by the choices you make, the actions you take, and the impact you have on the world around you. Every time you step up to a challenge, take responsibility, or choose growth over comfort, you are stepping into your calling. And with every step, that calling begins to take shape.

At any given moment, you have the chance to choose who you're becoming. You don't need to have the full map laid out in front of you. You just need to start moving forward. You'll learn as you go. Clarity comes through action, not waiting. Your purpose will reveal itself over time—but only if you're bold enough to take that first step, even when it feels uncertain.

It doesn't matter if that step is small. It doesn't matter if your voice shakes or your hands are unsure. What matters is that you move. Because movement is momentum, and momentum is what separates dreams from reality.

You may not always feel ready. You might doubt yourself or wonder if you're capable. But no one who ever built something meaningful started with full confidence. Every man who's ever made an impact began with some uncertainty. The difference is, they moved anyway. They acted in faith, not because they were fearless, but because they were committed.

You were made for more than just existing. You were created for something greater than drifting through life. Your calling isn't some mystery to solve—it's a journey to walk. And the more you walk it, the clearer it becomes.

So don't wait for perfect timing. Don't wait to feel ready. Step forward with what you've got. Do it with courage. Do it with intention. That's how you create a life of meaning—and step fully into the man you were meant to be.

◇◇◇◇◇

💬 Reflection
When have you hesitated instead of acting? What held you back, and what could have changed if you had stepped forward?

📓 Something to Write About
What's one step you can take today, no matter how small, that will bring you closer to your calling?

✖ Challenge
Choose one thing you've been avoiding. Take the first step toward it today—even if it's small or imperfect.

⊘ Code to Remember
Choose one thing you've been avoiding. Take the first step toward it today—even if it's small or imperfect.

13

Life Won't Be Easy. Choose It Anyway.

'You don't get to choose how hard life will be. But you do get to choose the kind of man you'll be when life gets hard.'

There's no version of life where everything runs smoothly, stays comfortable, and always goes your way. Pain, loss, pressure, and uncertainty are part of being human. The sooner you accept that, the sooner you can stop running from reality and start rising to meet it.

Most people spend their lives hoping things will get easier. They wait for the stress to fade before making a move. They put things off, thinking the right time will magically show up. Some blame others, some avoid taking ownership, and many stay stuck—wishing their circumstances would change without ever changing themselves.

But if you want to become the kind of man who leads, protects, builds, and inspires—you can't afford that mindset. Life will never hand you an ideal path. You have to stop waiting for it to get easy. Because it won't. And the longer you wait, the further you drift from the man you're meant to become.

Here's the good news: you don't need easy. You need something real. Because real life, with all its pressure and unpredictability, is what forges real strength. The struggles you didn't choose but still faced—the times you kept going when you wanted to quit—those are the moments that shape your character.

Each time you step up—when it's hard, when it's uncomfortable, when everything in you wants to tap out—you build something solid inside yourself. You prove that you're not here to be passive. You're here to become capable. Reliable. Strong. That kind of man is rare—and becoming one starts by embracing the challenge.

Don't waste your time wishing for less weight to carry. Train your back to carry more. Stop looking for the easy road and start walking the meaningful one. Choose the path that stretches you, sharpens you, and demands your full strength. Not because it's easy—but because it matters deeply.

When you commit to that kind of life, you stop running from difficulty—and start becoming the man you were meant to be.

◇◇◇◇◇

Reflection
What's one area of your life where you've been waiting for things to get easier before taking action?

Something to Write About
Write about a hard experience that made you stronger. What did it teach you about yourself?

Challenge
Pick one difficult task or responsibility you've been avoiding. Do it today—not because it's easy, but because it's worth it.

Code to Remember
I will not wait for life to get easier. I will show up and lead with strength—no matter how hard it gets.

14

Every Knight Must Face His Dragons

◇◇◇◇◇

'You can't conquer what you won't face. Each step toward fear shapes the man you're becoming.'

◇◇◇◇◇

There's a reason every old story about a hero includes a dragon. Not because fire-breathing beasts are real—but because fear is. Every man, at some point in his life, will face something that makes him want to run. It could be rejection, shame, pressure, doubt, or the fear of failure. These are your dragons. And there's no getting around the fact that every man will encounter them on his journey.

Dragons don't live in dark caves or remote places. They show up in your life's defining moments. They're there when you want to speak up but remain silent. They're there when it's easier to quit than to keep going. They're there when doing the right thing will cost you something, whether it's comfort, reputation, or even relationships. That's when your courage gets tested, and the choice you make—whether to face the fear or run from it—shapes you into who you'll become.

Avoiding the dragon doesn't make it go away. In fact, it only makes it grow stronger. Every time you turn your back on fear, it takes root and feeds on your hesitation. But every time you stand in the face of fear, even if your hands shake or your heart pounds, you become stronger. You develop the kind of quiet, unshakeable confidence that comes from knowing you've stood up to fear and survived. It's the kind of strength that says, 'I've been through worse, and I'm still standing.'

Real courage isn't loud. It doesn't always come with a grand gesture or a battle cry. Sometimes, it's simply showing up. Tired. Unsure. Scared. But still showing up. You won't always feel ready, but the key to growth is choosing to act anyway, even when you're not fully prepared.

Every knight earns his armour through struggle—by walking through fire, fighting battles no one sees. What separates boys from men isn't age or strength, but the decision to face difficulty head-on.

Don't wait for fear to fade. Don't wait for the perfect moment. Step forward toward what scares you. That's how knights are made—not by avoiding dragons, but by stepping into the cave and never turning back.

◇◇◇◇◇

💬 Reflection
What is one dragon you've been avoiding? What's the cost of not facing it?

📓 Something to Write About
Write about a moment when you showed courage—even when you were afraid. What did it teach you?

⚔ Challenge
Pick one fear and take real action this week—however small. The goal isn't to feel brave. It's to be brave.

🧭 Code to Remember
I will face what scares me, because that's how I become the man I was born to be.

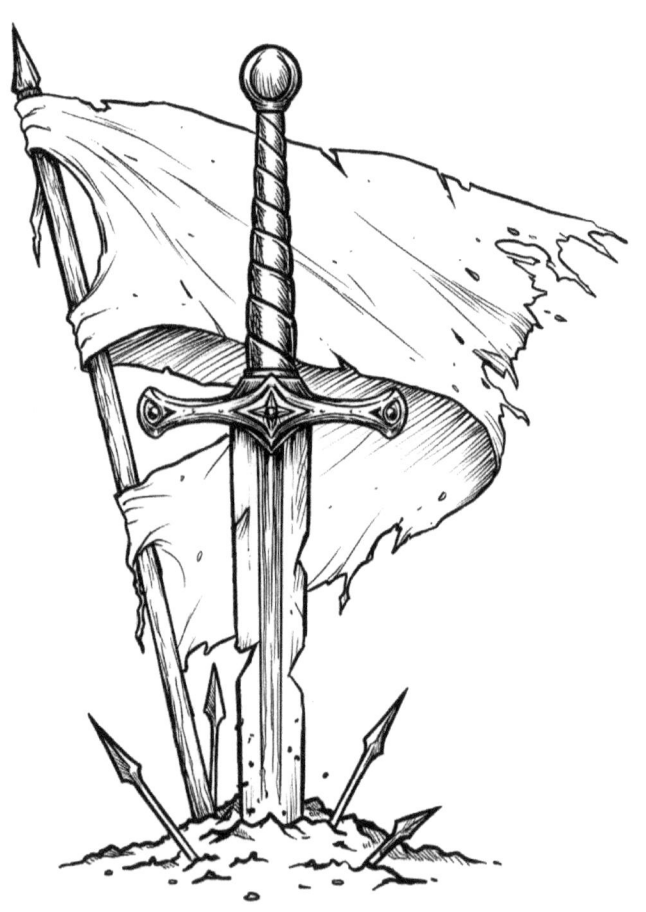

PART VII

Holding Your Ground with Honour

Throughout your life, there's going to be a lot of noise out there—telling you what to be, how to act, and what matters. But manhood isn't found in trends. It's built on truth.

This part will help you block out the distractions, stand firm in your values, and walk your path with clarity and strength. You'll learn to lead, not follow—to live with conviction, not for applause, and to be the same man in every space.

Because real strength doesn't need to shout to be heard.

1

Being Strong Doesn't Mean Being Cold

◇◇◇◇◇

'You don't have to shut off your heart to become strong. Real strength is choosing not to be hardened by the world—even when it tries to break you.'

◇◇◇◇◇

Sometimes, you might hear guys around you say that to be a strong man, you've got to be cold. Emotionless. Unbothered. As if nothing ever touches you. Let me be the one to tell you that this is an absolute myth. Real strength doesn't mean shutting off your emotions or walking through life with a blank stare. That's not toughness—that's numbness, and it doesn't serve anyone, least of all you.

True strength is about being able to feel everything, every bit of pain, every emotion, and still choosing to stand tall. It's about being hurt, yet still showing up when it counts. It's being kind without allowing others to walk all over you. It's speaking the truth, even when your voice shakes.

Coldness, more often than not, is just a shield—a defence mechanism some men use to hide fear, confusion, or the overwhelming weight of life's challenges. But pretending that nothing affects you doesn't make you strong—it just disconnects you from the world and the people around you.

You're not meant to become a robot. You're meant to become a man. A man who knows how to feel deeply without being ruled by those feelings. Strength doesn't come from shutting down, it comes from being steady, even when life throws you curveballs. It's about finding the balance of being grounded and open, brave and compassionate. You can be strong and still allow yourself to experience the full spectrum of life's emotions. Strength is not about closing yourself off—it's about staying open, even when the world makes it easy to shut down and pull away.

One day, you'll realise that the most powerful men you know are often the warmest. They don't shy away from their emotions—they just don't let them control their actions or define them. These men are solid, not because they act hard, but because their strength comes from a deep inner peace that doesn't need to put up walls.

Let the world see your strength, not through coldness, but through courage, clarity, and care. That's how truly strong men move through life.

◇◇◇◇◇

💬 Reflection:
What do you think some people get wrong about what it means to be strong?

📓 Something to Write About:
Write about a time you felt something deeply—but tried to hide it. What would it have looked like to show strength and emotion in that moment?

⚔ Challenge:
This week, practise speaking honestly about something you feel—without pretending you're fine when you're not.

🧭 Code to Remember:
I will be strong without becoming cold. I will feel, speak, and act with courage and control.

2

Masculinity Is Not the Problem—Lack of Guidance Is

◇◇◇◇◇

'Masculinity isn't dangerous. But when it's left unguided, it can lose its way. What you need isn't less strength—it's better direction.'

◇◇◇◇◇

Throughout your life, you may sometimes come across people trying to tell young men that masculinity is the problem—for a lot of things. That being strong, confident, or driven somehow makes you a threat to others. And this is absolutely insane to think. Because the truth is that masculinity, at its core, isn't harmful. It's not toxic. It's not wrong. It just needs direction and purpose. When misunderstood or left untended, it can become distorted. But when harnessed, it can create strength, respect, and wisdom.

Think of masculinity like a sword—it can either defend or destroy. It's the one holding it who determines its use. Your strength, ambition, and drive are the same. If left unchecked or without proper guidance, they can become dangerous, destructive, or self-serving. However, with discipline, respect, and a clear purpose, those same traits can be used to protect, to build, and to serve others.

The real problem isn't masculinity itself. The problem lies in the lack of strong men who are willing to guide and teach the next generation how to use their natural gifts. Too many young guys are given conflicting advice: either to tone themselves down or to unleash their energy without control. Neither of these paths leads to honour or true strength. What young men need is mentorship, a code to follow, and a reason to grow—not to hold themselves back, or become something they're not, but to become better at being the man they're meant to be.

It takes true courage to step up and say: 'I'm going to learn how to lead, protect, serve, and grow—not just with strength, but with wisdom.' That's the essence of healthy masculinity. It's not about being loud or reckless, but being grounded, steady, and directed toward something far greater than yourself.

Don't buy into the false choice that says you have to choose between being powerful and being good. You can—and should—be both. In fact, that's the whole point of becoming a man.

◇◇◇◇◇

▤ Reflection:
Why do you think some people view masculinity as a problem today?

📓 Something to Write About:
Who are the men—real or fictional—you've looked up to? What made their strength honourable?

✘ Challenge:
Pick one area of your life where you've acted with strength but not with direction. This week, take one step toward using that strength for something better.

❂ Code to Remember:
I will grow into a man of strength and purpose—one who leads, protects, and serves with honour.

3

What Real Confidence Looks Like

◇◇◇◇◇

'Real confidence isn't loud. It doesn't need to be. It comes from knowing who you are and standing firm, no matter what.'

◇◇◇◇◇

Confidence is one of the most misunderstood traits in young men. Too often, it gets confused with arrogance—showing off, being loud, acting like you're better than everyone else. But real confidence? It's quieter than that. It's stronger, more enduring, and far more valuable.

Real confidence means you don't have to prove anything to anyone. You don't need constant approval. You don't need to be the loudest guy in the room or constantly seek the spotlight. Confidence comes from within, from knowing who you are, what you stand for, and what you're working towards. It's not about showing off; it's about being grounded in your own values and vision for your life.

Confidence isn't about pretending you've got it all figured out, either. It's built through consistent action. It grows when you start keeping promises to yourself. When you say you'll do something—and then actually do it.

Whether that's waking up early, setting a boundary with someone, pushing through a tough workout, or owning your mistakes, each time you follow through, you build trust with yourself. That trust is the foundation of real confidence.

The most confident men aren't the ones who constantly brag about their wins or seek approval. They're the ones who stand alone when necessary, speak honestly, and stay consistent—guided by their own internal compass. Their confidence doesn't depend on applause from others. They know exactly who they are, and that's more than enough.

If you want to build confidence, start by doing the hard things without making a scene. Train in silence, where no one else can see your effort. Work with focus, not for praise. Speak with honesty, not for approval. And show up with integrity, even when no one notices.

You don't need the world to tell you you're enough. Start showing yourself. Let your actions speak louder than your words. The confidence you build today will carry you further than any external validation ever could.

◇◇◇◇◇

Reflection:
Where in your life do you rely on other people's approval to feel good about yourself?

Something to Write About:
Describe a time when you acted with quiet confidence. What did it feel like—and what did it change?

Challenge:
This week, do one difficult thing without announcing it or looking for praise. Let your actions speak.

Code to Remember:
I will build my confidence by keeping my word, facing what's hard, and staying true to who I am.

4

Don't Chase Girls. Build Yourself and Lead.

◇◇◇◇◇

'When you chase what runs, you lose sight of where you're going. Focus on your mission, and the right people will walk beside you.'

◇◇◇◇◇

From a young age, most guys are taught that being a man is all about attention—getting girls, being liked, and proving how wanted you are. But to be honest, chasing girls isn't strength. It's a distraction. You don't build real confidence by chasing approval from others. You build it by chasing something far greater—purpose and meaning.

If all your energy is focused on impressing others, you're not leading; you're following. You're shaping yourself based on what you think will get you noticed, and in doing that, you're losing sight of what really matters: becoming the kind of man who doesn't need to be flashy to be respected.

A man on a mission doesn't need to prove anything to anyone. He focuses on his own growth. He puts in the work without an audience. He trains his body, sharpens his mind, keeps his word, and builds a life he can stand on. That kind of presence speaks louder than any attempt at impressing someone. When you're focused on becoming the best version of yourself, the right people will notice. And the right girl will be drawn to you—not because you chased her, but because you didn't need to. You'll attract respect through action, not by seeking validation.

Stop asking if someone likes you. Instead, ask yourself if you like who you're becoming. Are you living in a way that earns your own respect? Are you building the kind of life that reflects the man you want to be? That's the foundation. That's the path to follow, and it will make you stronger, more confident, and ready for what's ahead.

Chasing girls may feel like everything now, but trust me—it fades. It really does. Becoming a man of value, though? That's what lasts. It's what gives you lasting strength, respect, and purpose. Focus on building yourself, and everything else will follow.

◇◇◇◇◇

💬 Reflection:
Are you spending more time trying to be noticed than becoming someone worth noticing?

📕 Something to Write About:
What would change in your daily life if you stopped chasing approval and started chasing excellence?

⚔ Challenge:
For the next seven days, redirect your focus. Every time you feel the urge to impress, shift it into improving a skill, building discipline, or finishing something you've been putting off.

❷ Code to Remember:
I won't chase what distracts me. I'll build a life of purpose, and let the right people be drawn to my direction.

5

Your Body Is a Tool, Not a Trophy

◇◇◇◇◇

'Strength isn't built for the mirror—it's built for the moments that test you.'

◇◇◇◇◇

Somewhere along the line, people started treating their bodies like the main event. Like muscles and appearance were the whole measure of strength. But real strength? It isn't built for attention—it's built for purpose. Your body isn't a trophy. It's a tool. It's what helps you show up, stand firm, and carry what needs carrying.

There's nothing wrong with looking good. But that shouldn't be your main focus. You don't train just to be admired—you train to be ready. Ready when someone's in danger. Ready when the work is heavy. Ready when your back's against the wall and there's no one else to step up. In those moments, your body doesn't need to impress anyone—it needs to endure.

A strong body sharpens the mind. It builds patience, grit, and emotional control. It gives you a place to put stress, a way to hold steady when life starts shaking. Whether strength comes naturally or through struggle isn't the point. What matters is that you earn it—through effort, through repetition, through refusing to quit when it gets uncomfortable.

Training isn't just about muscle. It's about mindset. It's where you learn to keep going when everything in you wants to stop. That kind of discipline doesn't stay in the gym—it follows you into every part of your life. Into how you work, how you lead, and how you respond when pressure rises and people are counting on you.

Yes, you can take pride in how you look. That's fine. But your strength should always serve something more. Because one day, someone will need you to lift something heavier than weights—responsibility, protection, leadership, pressure. And you'll either be the man who can carry it... or the one who breaks beneath it.

So train with purpose. Train like someone is counting on you—because one day, they will be. Build more than a body. Build a foundation. Build a man who's prepared, who leads, who lasts.

Be the man others lean on when everything is on the line.
The one who's ready when no one else is.

That's the kind of strength the world needs more of—the kind that holds the line when it counts.

◇◇◇◇◇

▣ Reflection:
Are you building your body for appearance—or preparing it for the challenges life will bring?

▦ Something to Write About:
Describe a situation where physical strength—or the lack of it—made a real difference.

✘ Challenge:
This week, train with purpose in mind. Ask yourself before every session: What am I building this strength for?

◉ Code to Remember:
I'll treat my body with respect—not for praise, but to be strong for what life demands.

6

Find Your Voice in a World Full of Noise

◇◇◇◇◇

'The loudest voices aren't always the wisest. Sometimes, the truth whispers—you just have to be quiet enough to hear it.'

◇◇◇◇◇

The world is full of noise. Everyone has something to say about what you should do, who you should be, and what you should want. Everywhere you turn, there's a new trend, a new opinion, or a new distraction pulling at your attention. If you're constantly listening to these external voices, you'll never hear your own. It's like trying to hear your thoughts in a room full of shouting, where every voice is trying to drown out the next. The pressure to conform is overwhelming.

Just like you learnt to focus your attention when you wanted to escape in *Part II, Day 12*, now you need to shift that focus inward. When you quiet the distractions around you, you create space for something much more important—yourself. You don't have to shut the world out completely, but you do need to carve out moments where you can hear your own thoughts, desires, and values. This is your opportunity to get clear about who you are and where you want to go, away from the noise that tries to cloud your vision and decisions.

The more you can tune out the external noise, the clearer your soul's voice becomes. It's like turning down the volume on everything else so you can hear the beat of your own rhythm. But this isn't easy. The temptation to let the world define you is powerful, especially when you're still figuring out who you are. The voices around you can pull you in a hundred different directions, leaving you unsure of where you stand, questioning your choices and your path. Don't let confusion hold you back.

Every moment you spend in stillness, reflection, or quiet is an opportunity to get closer to the truth of who you really are. It's in those quiet moments that you'll hear your inner direction—the pull toward your real purpose. Don't be afraid of silence. In it, you'll find clarity, strength, and a deeper understanding of yourself, which will empower you to move forward with confidence.

Remember, you can't always control the world around you, but you can control where you put your focus. In a world full of noise, you have the power to create silence within. And in that silence, your soul's voice will speak louder than anything else ever could.

◇◇◇◇◇

💬 Reflection
What's one area of your life where the noise around you has become too loud to hear your own thoughts?

📓 Something to Write About
Think about a time when you blocked out external distractions and listened to yourself. What did you learn about who you are?

✘ Challenge
Today, spend fifteen minutes in silence. No distractions. Just you, alone with your thoughts. See what comes up.

◉ Code to Remember
I will silence the world around me so I can hear the strength within me.

7

You Don't Have to Follow the Crowd

◇◇◇◇◇

'Crowds may cheer, but it's the few who choose their own path that change the world.'

◇◇◇◇◇

There's a lot of pressure to fit in. Whether it comes from school, your mates, or the world around you, it can feel like you're expected to act a certain way just to be accepted. But here's what I've learnt—blending in won't shape you into the man you're meant to become. It won't earn you respect. It won't build your character. It simply keeps you comfortable, and comfort rarely builds anything worth remembering.

Most people follow the crowd because it feels safer. It takes the weight off decision-making. You don't have to explain yourself, and you avoid standing out. But that safety comes with a price. When you follow the crowd, you give up a part of your voice. You start living someone else's story instead of writing your own.

Real growth doesn't happen when you take the easy road. It happens when you make decisions that match your values, even when those decisions aren't popular. That's where real strength lives—not in going along with the masses, but in choosing your own direction, even when no one else understands it.

Choosing your own path takes guts. It means you might be misunderstood. You might feel isolated at times. But the men who shape the world—the ones people remember—are never the ones who blend in. They're the ones who had the courage to go against the grain, to question what everyone else accepted, and to live by something deeper than popularity or applause.

When you walk your own way, you show the world that you stand for something. You're not just another follower—you're a man with conviction. And that kind of clarity can't be bought. It has to be built, tested, and earned through hard choices.

So if you ever feel like you have to change who you are just to belong, pause and check yourself. Belonging shouldn't cost your values. You were never meant to just fit in. You were meant to rise, to lead, and to stand firm in who you are—regardless of who's paying attention.

◇◇◇◇◇

Reflection
What areas of your life do you feel pressure to fit in? How can you choose your own path in these situations?

Something to Write About
Think about a time you went against the crowd. How did it feel? Would you do it again? Why or why not?

Challenge
Today, choose one decision where you're tempted to follow the crowd. Step back and ask yourself: What would my true self want? Then act on it.

Code to Remember
I will walk my own path, no matter how difficult or lonely it may seem. I define my direction.

8

Popular Isn't Always Right

⋄⋄⋄⋄⋄

'Strength isn't found in simply following the crowd. It's forged in standing alone when the world says you should fit in.'

⋄⋄⋄⋄⋄

It's easy to follow the crowd. When everyone's doing the same thing, it can feel safe, like you're part of something bigger. Fitting in offers comfort. It spares you from awkward questions and uncomfortable moments. But just because something is popular doesn't make it right. In fact, what's popular is often the path of least resistance—and that's rarely where real strength or growth lives.

Think about the times in history when real change happened. The men and women who made a difference weren't chasing approval. They stood firm when it mattered. They spoke up when others stayed silent. They were mocked, ignored, or hated at first—but over time, they were remembered. Why? Because they stayed true to their convictions.

Popular opinion is often shallow, driven by fear, laziness, or the need to be liked. It shifts with the wind. What's popular today is forgotten tomorrow. But your integrity? That's something you carry with you for life.

Sometimes, following the crowd can hold you back from becoming who you're meant to be. It keeps you locked into the idea of 'just fitting in', where no one makes waves, and no one stands out. But men of substance don't hide in the crowd—they rise above it. They choose the harder path: the one that might cost them attention, but earns them respect.

You don't need everyone to like you. You need to like the man you see in the mirror. And that only happens when you choose what's right over what's popular. Listen to your gut. Trust your judgement. If something feels off, it probably is.

It's not about rebelling just to be different. It's about holding fast to your values, especially when they're tested. Standing alone might feel heavy—but it's how leaders are built.

Remember, true strength isn't loud—it's steady. It's found in the quiet moments when you choose character over comfort. So don't follow the crowd. Lead yourself.

◇◇◇◇◇

💬 Reflection
When have you chosen to go against the grain? What motivated you to stand firm in your beliefs, even when it wasn't popular?

📓 Something to Write About
Describe a time when following the crowd held you back or led to a negative outcome. What would have happened if you'd chosen your own path instead?

⚔ Challenge
Today, identify one situation where you feel the pressure to conform. Take a stand, make the choice that aligns with your values, and see how it feels to resist the pull of the crowd.

● Code to Remember
I will forge my strength by standing firm in my beliefs, not by following the crowd.

9

The World Will Try to Shape You—Don't Let It

◇◇◇◇◇

'Don't let the world decide your identity. You are who you choose to be.'

◇◇◇◇◇

The world will always try to shape you, label you, and tell you who you should be. It pushes its own version of strength, of success, of what it means to be a man. But just because the crowd moves in one direction doesn't mean you need to follow. Standing apart takes courage—but it also builds character. Fitting in might seem easier in the moment, but it often comes at the cost of who you truly are.

You've already learnt from Day 1 that people will throw labels at you, trying to make you fit their idea of who you should be. Some will call you quiet when you're simply thinking. Others will say you're too serious, too intense, too emotional, too proud. Some may even call you weak when you show restraint, or strange when you refuse to lower your standards. But none of that defines you. You are who you decide to become.

The pressure to blend in is everywhere. Social circles, classrooms, media, even family at times—it can feel like you're being pulled in different directions. But real strength lies in resisting that pull. Choosing your values over popularity. Choosing your standards over comfort. Choosing your own path, even when you have to walk it alone.

Being different doesn't mean you're lost—it means you're on a path few are brave enough to walk. You don't need permission to be who you are. What you need is the courage to keep showing up as yourself when it would be easier not to.

The world will try to shape you into something smaller, something more manageable. But you get to shape yourself. With every decision, every action, every moment of resistance—you carve out the man you're becoming.

Don't let the world reduce you. Build yourself into something solid. Let the strength within speak louder than the noise outside.

◇◇◇◇◇

💬 Reflection
What are the outside pressures you feel most often? How do they try to shape you?

📓 Something to Write About
Think about a time when you resisted the pressure to fit in. How did it make you feel, and what did you learn about yourself?

✘ Challenge
Today, choose one area where you've been letting the world shape you. Take one step towards defining yourself instead—whether that's standing firm in your beliefs or making a choice that aligns with your values.

🧭 Code to Remember
I will resist the pressure to conform and choose the man I am becoming.

10

Be the Same Man Everywhere You Go

◇◇◇◇◇

'The character you build in the real world is the same character you show in every situation.'

◇◇◇◇◇

In life, it's easy to think of certain spaces as separate from who you are. You might feel like you can be someone different in certain settings—putting on a mask, shifting your tone, or adjusting your behaviour to fit in. But let's be clear: the man you are should never depend on where you are. Whether you're in a conversation, a meeting, at home, or walking alone—your values, your integrity, your actions—should stay the same. True integrity means alignment. It means living in a way that doesn't change based on your surroundings.

It can be tempting to adapt to gain approval or avoid conflict. But the more you do that, the more disconnected you become from the man you're trying to build. Every time you say one thing and do another, or act differently depending on who's watching, you chip away at your foundation. That fracture in your identity may seem small at first, but over time, it erodes your confidence and sense of self.

Authenticity doesn't just matter in public—it matters in private. The man you are behind closed doors should be the same man you are when the world is watching. That kind of consistency builds trust, both with others and with yourself. It creates a life without contradiction—a life where you don't have to look over your shoulder or remember which version of yourself you presented to which crowd.

Being true to yourself is a kind of strength most people underestimate.

It's not about being stubborn or inflexible—it's about being anchored. People respect those who stand firm, who speak honestly, and who act in alignment with what they believe.

So when the pressure comes to blend in, perform, or compromise, ask yourself: Is this still me? Is this who I want to be when I look back ten years from now?

It's not about being perfect—it's about being whole. When you live as the same man everywhere you go, you don't just earn respect—you earn peace.

◇◇◇◇◇

▣ Reflection
Do you feel like your actions match your values in every setting? Why or why not?

▦ Something to Write About
Write about a time when you acted differently depending on the situation. How did that feel, and what would you have done differently?

✗ Challenge
For the next twenty-hour hours, be intentional about showing up as the same person, no matter where you are or who you're with.

➋ Code to Remember
I will show up as my true self, in every situation, because integrity builds trust and respect.

11

Choose Character Over Recognition

◇◇◇◇◇

'Recognition fades, but character lasts an eternity.'

◇◇◇◇◇

When you're out in the world, it's easy to get caught up in the pursuit of recognition. You'll notice that a lot of people are obsessed with gaining attention, seeking validation, and being seen. It's tempting to measure your worth by how many people notice you. But the reality is, that type of recognition is temporary. It comes and goes with the tides of trends, popularity, and public approval. What's admired today might be forgotten tomorrow.

Character, however, doesn't fade. It's the quiet force that carries you through the ups and downs of life. When the spotlight moves on, character remains. It's the measure of a man that's never out of style, never replaced by trends, and never bought with influence. It's earned by your actions, your choices, and your ability to stay true to who you are—whether people are watching or not.

So, what does it mean to choose character over recognition? It means you don't chase after the applause of others. As I've mentioned throughout this book, you focus on doing the right thing, even when no one's watching. You make decisions that align with your values, not the latest popular opinion or what will get you the most attention. It's about being a man of integrity, even when the world around you is more focused on appearance than substance. When you live with character, you show up as your true self, unapologetically, day in and day out.

Real strength lies in your ability to stand firm in who you are and what you believe, even when it's inconvenient. It's easy to chase recognition, to give in to the pressure to be popular or liked. But true respect comes from your character. The more you choose integrity over shortcuts, the more people will begin to see the strength of your character. And ultimately, it's not others who define you—it's the man you are in your unguarded moments that matters most.

And trust me, that's what builds a lasting legacy. A legacy that's not based on trends, but on something real. A legacy built on the man you are, not the one you pretend to be. Character is the foundation of everything you'll leave behind.

◇◇◇◇◇

▥ Reflection
When was a time you made a decision based on what was right, even when it wasn't the easiest choice?

▌ Something to Write About
Describe an instance when you chose integrity over popularity. What was the outcome? How did it make you feel?

✘ Challenge
Today, make a choice that aligns with your character, not your desire for approval. It could be in how you speak, act, or even choose what you stand for. Do what's right, not what's easy.

❷ Code to Remember
I will focus on building my character and standing by what's right, even when it's not the easy choice.

12

Honour Doesn't Follow the Crowd—But It Lasts

◇◇◇◇◇

'Honour is who you are when no one's looking—and when no one will ever know.'

◇◇◇◇◇

Honour isn't something that shifts with opinion or fades with time. It's not built on what's popular or easy. Honour is a constant—a quiet strength that lives in the choices you make when only you know. It's doing what is right, not because it's seen, but because it's right.

The world often rewards the quick, the loud, and the easy. But that kind of attention fades. Honour may not always bring applause, and at times it might feel like a lonely road. But that's exactly what makes it powerful. The men who leave a lasting impact are not the ones who chase approval—they're the ones who walk with integrity when it's hardest to do so. They choose the harder right over the easier wrong, even when no one would fault them for taking the easy way out.

Think about the men you respect most. They didn't earn that respect by blending in. They earned it by staying true to what they believed in, even when it cost them something. Honour doesn't bow to pressure. It doesn't change shape to fit in. It stands firm.

Some days, honour looks like telling the truth when it would be easier to lie. Other times, it's owning your mistakes, treating someone with respect even if they don't deserve it, or holding back when you have the power to hurt. It's found in small, consistent decisions that shape your reputation and your character. And those small decisions, made repeatedly, become the habits that define who you are.

Being a man of honour isn't just about the big moments. It's shown in how you treat others, how you speak, how you carry yourself—especially when no one's around. Every time you choose honour over comfort, you lay another stone in the foundation of the man you're becoming.

The world may forget who was the loudest or the most liked. But it never forgets the man who stood for something.

Approval will always eventually fade. But honour?
Honour stays—echoing in the silence that follows, far beyond the applause, far beyond attention, and far beyond the moment... when all that remains is character.

◇◇◇◇◇

▣ Reflection:
Where in your life do you feel pressure to fit in or compromise your values? How can you stand firmer in those moments?

▤ Something to Write About:
Write about a time when you did the right thing even though it was difficult. How did it feel in the moment—and how do you feel about it now?

✖ Challenge:
Choose one area this week—school, home, friendships—where you'll practise honour, even when it's hard. Then do it quietly, without telling anyone.

◉ Code to Remember:
I will choose integrity over approval, honour over popularity.

13

The Power of Silence: Strength in Restraint

◇◇◇◇◇

'Silence is not the absence of sound, but the presence of power.'

◇◇◇◇◇

The world is loud. Opinions, distractions, and constant noise fight for your attention every second. There's pressure to react, respond, and always be visible. But in the middle of all that chaos, there's a quiet strength most people overlook: silence.

Silence is not weakness. It's not about running from difficulty or shutting down. It's about control. Focus. Power. When you choose silence, you reclaim your mind from the noise. You filter out what doesn't matter, so you can hear what does.

In those still moments, your thinking sharpens. You gain clarity. You see your next step with more precision. While others rush to speak, the silent man waits—observes—considers. His restraint is his strength.

The quiet man isn't empty. He's measured. He doesn't need to prove himself with constant noise. Instead, he lets his presence, choices, and actions speak louder than words ever could. He listens more than he talks, and when he finally speaks—people listen.

Holding your tongue when emotions run high takes discipline. It shows you're not ruled by ego or impulse. In arguments, in pressure, in tension—silence gives you space to respond with wisdom instead of regret. It's not just about saying less—it's about thinking more.

Sometimes silence is leadership. Sometimes, it's protection. Sometimes, it's how you keep your peace while everyone else is burning out trying to be heard. The man who can stay grounded when others spiral is the one others turn to when things fall apart.

Silence also lets you listen to your own conscience—your internal compass. Without it, you risk being shaped by the loudest voice in the room, instead of your own convictions. True growth often happens when no one else is around, and all that's left is you, your thoughts, and your choices.

Remember: silence isn't passivity—it's preparation. It's composure under fire. It's strength that doesn't need to shout. So practise it. Use it. Master it. Because the man who learns to control his silence can master everything else.

◇◇◇◇◇

💬 Reflection
When was the last time you chose silence over speaking? How did it impact the situation or the people around you?

📝 Something to Write About
Think of a moment when you used silence to your advantage. What was the outcome, and what did you learn from it?

✘ Challenge
The next time you feel the urge to speak in a tense situation, take a moment of silence instead.

⊘ Code to Remember
I will embrace the power of silence, knowing that true strength often lies in restraint and quiet contemplation.

14

Be the Example You Wish You'd Had

'The best way to lead is by example, not by instruction.'

When you're the kind of man you respect, you don't need to tell others how to act—you show them. Real leadership isn't about giving orders or demanding respect; it's about living the example. It's quiet, steady, and built on how you carry yourself when it matters most—especially when no one's watching. People are drawn to those who walk with conviction, speak with purpose, and act with integrity.

This isn't about being flawless. It's about being *consistent*. The kind of consistency that doesn't waver under pressure. The kind that shows up early, does what's right, and owns every outcome.

When you strive to become the man you *wish* you'd had as a role model, you begin to fill a gap not only for yourself—but for those around you. Whether you realise it or not, someone is watching how you move through life. A younger sibling, a classmate, a friend. Maybe even someone you've never met, who just happened to notice the way you held your ground.

Leadership doesn't begin with giving advice. It begins with how you live. Your actions, your choices, your attitude—these speak louder than anything you could say. A true leader doesn't demand followers; he earns their trust through grit, character, and quiet strength.

This kind of leadership is built in the small, often unnoticed moments.

Helping someone without being asked. Admitting when you're wrong. Choosing discipline over comfort. These things add up.

And while it may feel thankless at times, know this—you are setting a standard. A standard that others will measure themselves against. One day, someone will face a hard choice and think, 'What would he do?' That's the power of your example.

Lead without needing recognition. Be the man others can rely on. Your example is your legacy—and the more honourable and intentional it is, the more lives it will quietly change.

◇◇◇◇◇

💬 Reflection
Think about a time when you were inspired by someone's example. What qualities did they demonstrate that you can embody in your own life?

📓 Something to Write About
Write about a time when you had the opportunity to set an example for someone else. How did you handle it, and what did you learn from the experience?

⚔ Challenge
In the coming days, focus on leading others through your actions. Whether at home, school, or work, make choices that align with your values and be mindful of the message you're sending by the example you set.

⊘ Code to Remember
I will lead by example, knowing that my actions speak louder than my words, and I will be the kind of man others can look up to.

PART VIII

Becoming the Man You're Meant to Be

You're not just growing—you're stepping into the man you were meant to be. Every choice you make in your life, every step you take, and every challenge you face, is shaping the man you'll one day become.

This part is about owning that journey. It's time to step up, build your life with purpose, and live in a way that leaves a legacy now—not someday. You'll learn to lead yourself, serve others, and carry strength with kindness.

Because the man you're becoming? He's built by what you do today.

1

Start Becoming the Man You Would Look Up To

◇◇◇◇◇

'You don't become a man you admire by accident. You build him— one choice, one action, one day at a time.'

◇◇◇◇◇

There's a question that can anchor your life—one you should ask yourself often: Would I admire the man I'm becoming? It's a hard question to dodge when you're honest. It forces you to confront yourself on a deeper level, making you reflect on how you show up when no one's watching, how you treat people who can't benefit you, and how disciplined you are with your time, words, and actions.

Every decision, no matter how small, is shaping you into someone you'd either look up to... or someone you wouldn't trust with your story.

This isn't just about big moments—it's about the everyday actions. When you choose integrity over convenience, when you choose to follow through even when the world isn't watching, that's when you build the character that commands respect. You're not just building your reputation; you're building your legacy. The man you're becoming is a product of the decisions you make each and every day.

Back in Part IV, you learnt about the value of learning from those who've walked ahead. But now? It's your turn to start becoming that man for someone else—whether you realise it yet or not. You never know who's watching. You never know when your quiet consistency, your resilience, or the way you carry yourself might give someone else the permission to rise, to keep going, or to finally step up and be the best version of themselves.

The man you admire likely has integrity. He keeps his word. He owns his mistakes. He protects what's right, stands firm in discomfort, and leads by example. You can become him—but only if you stop waiting for life to shape you, and instead choose to shape yourself with purpose, every day.

It starts now. Not next year, not when you've figured everything out. Becoming the man you would admire doesn't require perfection—it requires daily effort, uncomfortable growth, and honest self-reflection. You won't always feel like it. But those are the moments that will define you.

◇◇◇◇◇

Reflection
What traits do you admire most in others—and how often do you reflect those in your own life?

Something to Write About
List three men you look up to. What is it about how they live that earns your respect?

Challenge
For the next seven days, act as if a younger version of you is watching everything you do. Set the standard.

Code to Remember
I will build the man I want to be through consistent choices, discipline, and integrity.

2

What Kind of Man Do You Want to Be by 21?

'If you don't decide who you want to become, someone else will decide for you.'

One day, you're going to be twenty-one years old, whether you plan for it or not. The real question is—what kind of man will show up? Way too many guys drift through their teens, thinking manhood will just happen one day. That it'll kick in when they hit a certain age, finish school, or start working.

But that's not how it works.

Manhood isn't something that magically appears; it's something you build—on purpose. It's not a destination, but a lifelong journey, and it starts with the choices you make right now. You're actively constructing the man you want to become each day.

You don't drift into strength. You don't coast into character. You choose to become the man you want to be—by showing up every single day, pushing through, and doing what most others won't. It's in the small actions, the consistent discipline, and the hard decisions, even when your only witness is yourself.

Each choice—every habit, every action, every decision—shapes the man you'll become. It's either building your future or quietly breaking it down. And if you're not clear about the man you want to become, you'll end up being shaped by whatever's around you: the noise, the pressure, the crowd.

Think back to *Part I, Day 9 – How to Become the Man You Look Up To*. That version of yourself—the one who walks with confidence, who's respected, who leads even when it's hard to do—he's not just some fantasy.

He's forged in the quiet moments. He's built by the choices you make now. When you train even when you don't feel like it. When you hold your ground instead of following the crowd. When you tell the truth, even when lying would be easier. These are the moments that shape you, when you push past comfort and stand for what you believe.

By twenty-one, the man you will be isn't a surprise. He's the sum of everything you've done to get there. Start building him now. The foundation starts today.

◇◇◇◇◇

💬 Reflection
What qualities do I want my twenty-one-year-old self to have—and am I building those qualities today?

📓 Something to Write About
Describe the man you hope to be at twenty-one. What habits, values, and traits define him?

✘ Challenge
Do one thing today that the man you're becoming would be proud of. Speak up, push through, or show up—then do it again tomorrow.

◉ Code to Remember
I will build the man I respect through the choices I make, to become a man worth admiring.

3

The Difference Between Impressing and Impacting

⋄⋄⋄⋄⋄

'Some men fade when the spotlight shifts. Others leave a mark that time never erases.'

⋄⋄⋄⋄⋄

There's a moment every young man reaches where he has to make a choice: will you chase the applause, or will you build a legacy?

Trying to impress others can feel powerful in the moment. You get the compliments, the followers, the recognition—and it feels good. But it fades—quickly. Because the spotlight always moves. Someone newer, louder, and flashier comes along. And if you've built your worth on being noticed, that silence can crush you. The applause is fleeting, and without something deeper, you're left with only the echo of your efforts, which can quickly feel hollow.

Impact, though? It's different. It's not about the fleeting admiration or external validation. It's about how you make people feel. It's about what you build, what you leave behind, and the difference you create in the lives of others. Impact happens when your presence lifts others up. When your words land because they come from a place of truth and integrity. When your actions resonate long after you've moved on, and those you've touched carry your example forward, creating ripples of influence beyond your awareness.

Think about the man we just talked about yesterday in *'What Kind of Man Do You Want to Be by 21?'*. Is he trying to be liked, constantly seeking approval—or is he living in a way that changes people for the better? The strongest men you'll meet aren't the loudest. They aren't the ones trying to win attention. They're the ones who do the quiet, consistent work—building respect, living their values, and making things better, day by day, even when their efforts go unnoticed.

There's absolutely nothing wrong with achieving great things or standing out. But if your only goal is attention, you'll always feel empty when the noise fades. If your goal is impact, you'll stay rooted and fulfilled—because your work matters, whether people are watching or not.

You won't always get applause for making a difference. But do it anyway.

◇◇◇◇◇

▭ Reflection
Are you building your life around being noticed—or making a real difference?

▬ Something to Write About
Write about someone who impacted you without trying to impress you. What made them different? How could you show up like that this week?

✗ Challenge
Do something impactful today without anyone knowing. No credit. No mention. Just service.

⊘ Code to Remember
I will aim to impact more than I impress.

4

Leave Every Space Better Than You Found It

⋄⋄⋄⋄⋄

'A strong man doesn't just pass through—he leaves things better behind him.'

⋄⋄⋄⋄⋄

Some guys go through life taking. Taking attention. Taking energy. Taking up space without giving anything back. But the men people remember—the ones who are respected—are the ones who build. The ones who step in and quietly leave things better than they found them.

It doesn't have to be dramatic. It could be as small as cleaning up after yourself, offering encouragement to a friend, or helping someone without being asked. Or it could be as big as launching something that benefits others long after you've moved on. It's not the size of the gesture—it's the mindset behind it.

You don't need money, titles, or permission to make an impact. What you need is awareness—and the decision to live as a builder, not just a consumer. Look around. What's one small thing you can improve about the space you're in right now? Is it your attitude? The energy you bring? A conversation that needs to be had? A standard you can raise?

Leaving things better isn't limited to physical spaces—it's every environment you touch. Your team. Your classroom. Your friendships. Your home. It's about recognising that your presence should add value. Not for applause, not for attention, but because that's who you're choosing to be.

Don't wait until you're older, more experienced, or in a position of leadership. Start now. With what's right in front of you. Every room you walk into, every conversation you're part of, every task you're handed—it's all an opportunity to leave something behind that's better than before.

Each time you take initiative, show care, or raise the standard, you're not just making a difference—you're becoming a man of influence. One who builds rather than breaks. One who gives rather than takes. One who leaves a legacy through quiet, consistent impact.

Some people leave a mess behind them. Be the man who leaves momentum.

◇◇◇◇◇

Reflection
What spaces in your life have you just been passing through instead of improving?

Something to Write About
Write down three ways you could leave a space—physical, relational, or emotional—better than you found it this week.

Challenge
Choose one of those ideas and act on it today. Don't explain it. Just do it.

Code to Remember
I will leave every space better than it was before I arrived, creating positive change for those who come after me.

5

You're Just Getting Started

◇◇◇◇◇

'Progress doesn't mean you're done—it means you're ready for what's next.'

◇◇◇◇◇

It's easy to get caught up in where you are right now—whether you feel ahead of others, behind, or just stuck in the same place. Ultimately, no matter where you stand on your journey, you're still only at the beginning. Life is a marathon, not a sprint. And everything you've done so far is just the groundwork for what's still to come.

Too many men fall into the trap of thinking they've 'arrived' once they reach a certain milestone—finishing school, landing a job, hitting the gym consistently, or even getting a bit of recognition. But that moment isn't the end. It's the start of the real work. Because after you've reached one peak, there's always another climb waiting. And those climbs will ask even more of you.

This is when you begin shaping the man you're meant to be. It's where your character is tested and forged. You begin to cement your values, to build habits that last, and to show the world who you truly are—not through your words, but through your consistency.

There's always more to learn. Always room to grow. More responsibilities, harder choices, tougher challenges. But that's the beauty of this path. Each step forward, each win, and even each mistake is part of the process. It's not about chasing perfection. It's about showing up and doing the work, again and again, no matter how you feel.

So stop obsessing over the finish line. Focus on your next step. The next challenge. The next time you get the chance to push through something hard. Growth doesn't come all at once—it comes from doing the small things with purpose, over and over.

If you want to leave a lasting mark, if you want to become a man others can count on, then you've got to keep showing up. Keep refining. Keep evolving. Even when no one notices. Even when it's tough.

You're not behind. You're not done.
You're just getting started.

⋄⋄⋄⋄⋄

Reflection
What's one area of your life where you've felt like you've 'arrived'? How can you shift your mindset to see it as just the beginning, rather than the end?

Something to Write About
Write down three ways you can continue growing in the next year. What's something new you can start working on to improve?

Challenge
Identify a skill, habit, or mindset you've been neglecting. Spend some time working on it today, even if just for 20 minutes.

Code to Remember
I will keep pushing forward, knowing that every step I take is part of the journey that shapes the man I will become.

6

Legacy Isn't Later—It's Now

'Every moment is a chance to lead by example—especially when no one's watching.'

A lot of guys think legacy is something for later. Something you worry about when you're older, once your career is settled or your life is more stable. But that's not how legacy works. You're building it right now, whether you realise it or not.

You're creating your legacy with every decision you make—every time you show up, every time you choose integrity when it would be easier not to. It's in the way you treat people. The way you speak. The example you set, especially when no one's watching. Even the smallest moments are shaping what others remember you for.

Legacy isn't just about big achievements—it's about how people feel after being around you. How you carry yourself when things are tough. How you respond when they go well. Do you build others up? Do you take responsibility for your actions? These little things stack up. They form a pattern. And that pattern becomes your reputation—your legacy in motion.

Here's the part no one tells you: the habits you build now will follow you. If you cut corners now, you'll do it later. If you avoid hard conversations now, they'll only get harder. But if you practise strength and character now, you'll be ready to lead when the time comes. You don't become a man of integrity by accident—you become one through repetition, through practice, through the little choices that most people overlook.

You don't have to wait until you're twenty or thirty to think about the man you want to be remembered as. Legacy isn't some far-off goal. It's right here, in how you show up for the people around you today. Every step, every choice, every standard you hold sends a message. Ask yourself honestly: If someone followed my lead today, where would I be taking them?

One day, someone will remember how you made them feel. Someone will repeat something you said, or follow a standard you set. That's legacy. You don't control everything about how people see you—but you do control the example you leave behind. Make it count.

◇◇◇◇◇

💬 Reflection:
What kind of legacy are you building today—through your words, your actions, and your example?

📓 Something to Write About:
Describe a man in your life whose example left a lasting mark on you. What specific things did he do that shaped your memory of him?

⚔ Challenge:
Be deliberate today. Speak with purpose. Carry yourself like someone is learning how to live by watching you—because they probably are.

🧭 Code to Remember:
I will treat every decision as a brick in the foundation of my legacy.

7

The World Needs the Gift Only You Can Bring

◇◇◇◇◇

'There is a unique gift inside you that the world has been waiting for—don't hold it back.'

◇◇◇◇◇

There's something in you that no one else has. A spark, entirely your own. A combination of your experiences, strengths, perspective, and drive—completely unique to you. That's your gift. It doesn't have to be flashy or loud, or win awards. Your ideas, your talents, and your unique perspective are essential—whether you recognise it or not.

Your gift might be a way of thinking, a talent in art or sport, an ability to care deeply, or the knack for inspiring others with your quiet strength. It's not something that everyone else has, and that is your power. When you share that gift, whether through your words, your actions, or the way you simply live your life, you make a difference in ways you may never fully comprehend. Sometimes that difference won't even be visible—but it will still matter.

The thing is, way too many guys hold back, thinking they need to become someone else before they can offer something of value. But the world doesn't need another copy. It needs your voice. Your example. Your courage. The way you show up and lead, even in small ways—that's your gift in action. Every time you choose to develop your strengths instead of hiding them, you make space for others to do the same.

You don't have to wait for someone to give you permission. You don't need to be the best in the room. What matters most is that you show up as yourself and keep showing up, especially when it's hard. That's where your impact grows.

Think of it this way: if you keep hiding what makes you special, you deny the world the opportunity to be enriched by it. The man who brings his unique gift into every space—be it a classroom, a team, or a friendship—is the man who leaves a lasting impact. That impact is built not on noise or showmanship, but on authenticity.

You might not always see the impact you're making, but someone needs what only you can give. So own it. Sharpen it. Share it.

◇◇◇◇

💬 Reflection:
When have you held back your true self, and how might the world have been different if you had shared your gift?

📓 Something to Write About:
Describe what you believe is your unique gift. How can you use it to make a positive impact on those around you?

🗡 Challenge:
Today, choose one way to share your gift—whether through a kind word, a creative act, or standing firm in your beliefs. Notice the effect it has on others.

⊙ Code to Remember:
I will share my unique gift boldly, knowing it is needed by the world.

8

Every Step You Take Is a Message to the Next Generation

◇◇◇◇◇

'Every step you take leaves a mark. Walk in a way that's worth following.'

◇◇◇◇◇

You're not just living for today—you're setting an example for tomorrow. The way you handle challenges, treat people, and carry yourself is shaping how others will do the same. Younger boys are watching. Your peers are noticing. Even adults pick up on how you show up. Whether you realise it or not, you're already influencing the people around you.

Every step you take sends a message: This is how a man walks through the world. So the question you should ask yourself is—what are your steps saying?

You don't have to be perfect. But you do need to be aware. Every choice you make, every time you speak up or stay silent, every moment you carry yourself with integrity (or don't), you're setting an example. That example could give someone else the courage to keep going, to choose better, to aim higher.

The next generation won't just learn from what you say. They'll remember what you did. The way you acted when things got hard. The way you treated people when you had nothing to gain. That's what they'll carry forward. Quiet moments of honesty, small acts of courage—those are the things that echo.

And this doesn't just apply to younger boys. You're influencing your peers, too. The men around you are also learning from your consistency, your character, and your values. You're shaping the standard of what it means to be a man in every space you enter.

Like we talked about back in *Part IV Day 13*, leadership isn't always about taking charge—it's about taking responsibility. True leadership starts with how you live, long before you ever get a title. You don't need to be the loudest or most popular. You just need to be consistent. Be real. Be someone worth following, even when no one gives you credit for it.

Your life speaks louder than your words ever could. Make your steps count—because someone out there is watching, learning, and following. And the legacy you leave will begin with how you walk today.

◇◇◇◇◇

💬 Reflection:
What message are your current actions sending to those who look up to you?

📓 Something to Write About:
Think of a man you've looked up to. What specific actions made him stand out?

✘ Challenge:
Choose one area of your life where someone younger is watching—school, sport, family. Take one intentional action this week that sets an example you'd be proud for them to follow.

🧭 Code to Remember:
I will lead by example and carry myself in a way worth following.

9

Be Proud of Who You See in the Mirror

◇◇◇◇◇

'A mirror doesn't measure your worth—it reflects the results of your choices. Make them count.'

◇◇◇◇◇

You see yourself every day—sometimes for a few seconds, sometimes longer. Whether you're brushing your teeth, tying your shoes, or just passing by a reflection, you're always facing the one person you can't lie to. No pretending. No fake smiles. Just you. And the question that matters most is this: are you proud of the guy looking back at you?

It's easy to worry about how other people see you—if you're cool enough, strong enough, popular enough. But h, absolutely none of that matters as much as how you see yourself. When it's quiet, when the crowd is gone, when no one's watching—are you proud of how you act? Do you respect the way you treat others? Are you someone, or becoming someone, you'd want to follow and be proud of?

You might not be exactly where you want to be yet—and that's okay. Growth takes time. But don't miss the small victories along the way. There's real strength in keeping your cool when it would've been easier to lash out. In choosing to do what's right when there's no spotlight shining on you. In staying true to what you believe, even if it means you're standing alone. All of these choices build character. These choices are the pieces of the man you're becoming.

So take a minute and look at how far you've already come. What are the things you've pushed through? What are the things you've learnt? What are the decisions you've made that have helped you grow stronger, kinder, wiser? The man in the mirror might not be perfect—but if he's trying, if he's honest, if he's doing the work—he deserves your respect. Because that kind of effort matters. It builds something solid inside you.

While it's always for people to recognise your efforts, you don't need applause to know you're doing well. The most important kind of pride is the kind that lives inside you—earned by the choices you make when no one else will ever know. That's real.

You're not here to impress people. You're here to become someone you can look in the eye and be proud of. So keep showing up. Keep doing the work. That version of you—the one who's real, steady, and strong—is the version worth becoming.

◇◇◇◇◇

💬 Reflection:
If you could only be judged by who you are when no one's watching, would you be proud of that version of yourself?

📓 Something to Write About:
What are three qualities you want to see in the man you're becoming? What are you doing today to build them?

⚔ Challenge:
Take five minutes to look yourself in the mirror. Be honest with yourself—are you proud of who you see? Make one decision today that will make the guy in the mirror proud.

⊘ Code to Remember:
I will live in a way that earns my own respect—so I can be proud of who I see in the mirror.

10

Write a Life Worth Reading

◇◇◇◇◇

'You are the author of your story. Every day is a chance to write the next chapter.'

◇◇◇◇◇

Your life is a story being written every single day, and you're the author. You hold the pen to your future. Every choice you make, every word you speak, every action you take—these shape the narrative you'll one day look back on. It's easy to feel like life is just happening to you, but is, you're making decisions constantly. The way you handle challenges, the people you keep close, the habits you maintain, and the standards you uphold—all of it is part of the story you're telling. So, what kind of story is it?

You don't control every event, but you do control your response. Setbacks, successes, and silent struggles all shape your character. Mistakes won't ruin your story—they're part of the journey. They bring lessons. They mark turning points. And like in any great story, the hard parts often reveal the most meaningful growth.

You are the main character in your life, and like any great story, growth comes from conflict, perseverance, and choice. The decisions you make today aren't just about getting through the day—they're shaping who you'll be next week, next year, and beyond. The habits you form now, the values you stand on, and the people you surround yourself with are writing your next chapter before it arrives.

Living a life worth reading isn't about chasing perfection—it's about owning your story and showing up with intention. You don't need to know how every chapter ends. Just keep writing. If today's page is messy, keep going. If you've stumbled, turn it. You're not stuck. You're still writing.

Don't wait for someone else to hand you the life you want. Create it. Don't wait for the perfect moment to start becoming the man you're meant to be—start now. You don't need permission to rewrite your path.

You can't erase the past, but you can take full ownership of what comes next. The pages ahead are still blank. What you write with them is entirely up to you.

So remember, you're the author of your story. Be sure to write a life worth reading.

◇◇◇◇◇

💬 Reflection
What kind of man do you want to become—and what values should shape your story from here?

🎟 Something to Write About
Write down three actions—big or small—you can take today to move closer to the man you want to be.

✘ Challenge
Start rewriting your story today. Take one of the actions you wrote down and take that first step, no matter how small.

❷ Code to Remember
I am the author of my story, and every choice I make shapes who I become.

11

Don't Just Live—Build a Life

⋄⋄⋄⋄⋄

'Life isn't just about existing—it's about creating something worth living for.'

⋄⋄⋄⋄⋄

You've been given the gift of time. It's your choice what you do with it. You can pass through your days on autopilot—just getting by—or you can step up and build a life that reflects who you are, what you believe in, and the legacy you want to leave behind. The difference between simply existing and intentionally building a life lies in your daily choices.

Building a life isn't passive. It requires hard work, discipline, and patience. It means setting goals that actually matter to you and staying consistent, even when motivation fades. You won't always feel like doing the right thing—but building anything meaningful requires action, not just good intentions.

It's easy to let time slip away while waiting for something external to change. But a life worth living doesn't fall into your lap. You build it—brick by brick, habit by habit, decision by decision. That means investing in your growth, building solid friendships, learning from your mistakes, and refusing to settle for a life that doesn't align with your values.

The reality is that no one is going to build your life for you. People can support you, teach you, or walk beside you—but you've got to do the heavy lifting. The kind of life you're proud to look back on isn't one you find. It's one you forge. Every lesson you learn, every challenge you face, and every time you get back up—these are the moments that shape the foundation of your future.

Ask yourself: What kind of life do I want to build? What kind of man do I need to become to live that life? Your future isn't waiting at some distant milestone. It starts today, with what you choose to do next.

Don't waste your days coasting through. Build something with your time, your energy, and your heart. Build a life that reflects your strength, your purpose, and your potential. A life worth waking up for. A life you'd be proud to call your own.

◇◇◇◇◇

💬 Reflection
Think about the life you're building right now. Are your actions and decisions aligning with the life you want to live? What changes can you make to move closer to that vision?

📓 Something to Write About
Write about the life you want to build in the next five years. What does that life look like? What steps can you take today to start moving toward it?

⚔ Challenge
Today, take one step—big or small—that moves you toward the life you want to build. This could be making a decision, starting a new habit, or reaching out to someone who can help you along the way.

🎯 Code to Remember
I will build a life that reflects my values, my purpose, and my vision.

12

Lead Yourself Before You Lead Others

◇◇◇◇◇

'True leadership begins with self-mastery. If you can't control yourself, you can't expect to guide others.'

◇◇◇◇◇

You've probably heard that leadership starts with the ability to lead yourself. It's not just a cliché—it's the foundation of being someone others can look to for guidance. If you can't control your thoughts, emotions, and actions, how can you expect to lead anyone else? Leadership isn't about having all the answers or being perfect; it's about self-mastery and making consistent choices that align with your values.

The battle within is the toughest fight you'll ever face. It's the internal struggle that no one else can see, but that you feel every day. It's the fight between who you are now and who you want to become, against doubts, fears, and the temptation to take the easy way out. If you can't win this battle, you won't be able to lead others effectively. Leadership begins by mastering yourself and making decisions that show others the way.

Before you can guide others, you need to master yourself. This means controlling your habits, thoughts, and emotions, and making the right choices even when no one is around to witness it. Self-discipline is the foundation of leadership—without it, others won't follow your example. Without self-discipline, there's no consistency, no foundation to build on. A leader who can't control himself will have difficulty inspiring others.

Leadership isn't about titles. It's about integrity, responsibility, and staying steady under pressure. To inspire those around you, conquer your own doubts and weaknesses. Leadership begins with making decisions in alignment with your values, even when the pressure is on. When you win the battle within, you'll be ready to help others. Your growth is the first step in their growth.

The battle within yourself is a daily one—and it never truly ends. Some days you'll win, others you'll struggle—but the key is never giving up. Keep fighting. Keep pushing forward. When you win this battle, you'll be ready to lead others, not by force, but by the strength of your example. True leadership starts from within.

◇◇◇◇◇

▰ Reflection
Think about the battles you face within yourself. What are the areas where you struggle the most? What can you do today to begin overcoming them?

▰ Something to Write About
Write about a time you overcame an internal struggle. What did you learn, and how can you apply that now?

✘ Challenge
Identify one area of your life where you're not fully in control. Make a plan to take ownership of that area and take one action step toward mastering it.

◉ Code to Remember
I will win the battle within by staying disciplined, being true to my values, and taking responsibility for my actions.

13

Strength and Kindness Can Coexist

◇◇◇◇◇

'You don't have to choose between being strong and being kind. The best leaders live both, every day.'

◇◇◇◇◇

There's a common belief that being strong means being cold, unfeeling, distant, or unshakably tough. But that version of strength is incomplete. Real strength isn't about putting up walls—it's about knowing who you are and choosing how to show up. A strong young man doesn't need to intimidate others to prove his worth. He earns respect through calm confidence and steady character.

Kindness isn't weakness. It takes more strength to show patience, empathy, and understanding when the easy choice would be to lash out or shut down. When you know your values and stand firm in them, you can offer kindness without fear of being walked over. Being kind when it's hard—when you're tired, frustrated, or misunderstood—shows the depth of your strength more than raising your voice ever could.

Real strength means using your presence to build, not break. It's about stepping in when someone needs protection, not just when there's something to prove. It's having the self-control to walk away from a pointless fight and the courage to step up when it actually counts.

The strongest people aren't always the loudest or the most aggressive—they're the ones who stay grounded and lead with integrity. They know when to speak up, when to listen, when to protect, and when to comfort. Strength without kindness turns into cruelty. Kindness without strength becomes passivity. But together, they build the kind of man others trust and admire.

You don't have to choose between being strong or being kind. The world needs more men who don't confuse harshness with power. It needs men who protect, serve, and lead with a steady hand and a solid heart. Kindness guided by strength is a powerful force. Never feel like you have to give one up to keep the other—they were meant to work together.

The most powerful version of you lives in the balance between the two. Show your strength not just in how you stand your ground, but in how you care for those around you. That balance is where real leadership begins.

◇◇◇◇◇

▣ Reflection
When things get tough, do you lean more toward strength or kindness? How can you balance both?

▣ Something to Write About
Write about a time when someone showed both strength and kindness. How did it affect you?

✘ Challenge
Find one moment today where you can show both strength and kindness. Take the opportunity to live both sides.

◉ Code to Remember
I will show that true strength includes kindness, and I will lead with both courage and compassion.

14

You Become the Man You Choose to Be— Every Day

◇◇◇◇◇

'Every decision you make shapes the man you're becoming. Choose the ones that build the future you want to live in.'

◇◇◇◇◇

The journey of becoming a man doesn't end with a lesson, a chapter, or even this book. It's built choice by choice, day by day. You don't wake up one morning as the man you've always wanted to be—you grow into him through your actions, your discipline, and your willingness to keep going when things get hard.

Every time you decide to do the right thing instead of the easy thing, you take a step forward. Every time you show up for yourself, keep your word, or push through discomfort, you shape who you're becoming. And when you mess up—and you will—that's another chance to learn, reset, and move forward stronger. You're not expected to be perfect. But you are responsible for trying again. The key is consistency. Not in being the best every day, but in choosing to return to your values—especially on the days when it's hardest.

Some days you'll feel off. You'll question your progress. That's part of the process. Growth is rarely loud or obvious—it's built in silence, in private moments, in the small decisions no one sees. That's where your character is forged. Anyone can act tough in front of a crowd, but real strength is who you are when no one's watching. Quiet discipline beats loud promises every time.

The man you become will not be shaped by comfort. He'll be shaped by pressure, by failure, and by your response to both. If you want to build a strong body, you need resistance. If you want to build a strong mind, you need challenges. And if you want to build a strong life, you need values you won't bend on—no matter what the world throws at you. You will be tested. But you won't be alone—brotherhood is built for this. Lean on it. Stand in it. Give back to it.

No one else can make these choices for you. Becoming a man of strength, honour, and purpose isn't something you inherit—it's something you earn through how you live. You're not just growing up. You're building a life. And that life starts with who you choose to be, again and again, in every moment.

In many ways, you are a modern knight. A knight doesn't need to wear armour, because his integrity, responsibility, and courage are his shield and sword. As a knight, you should always stand firm in your values, protect what's right, and lead by example. The challenges you face are your battlegrounds, and how you navigate them shapes you into a man others can count on. It's not about titles, medals, or banners; it's about honour, strength, and the choices you make every day.

You may not feel like a leader right now. You may still be figuring things out. That's totally normal. Because leadership isn't about having all the answers. It's about taking ownership of your actions, holding yourself to a higher standard, and lifting others up along the way. That's the kind of man this world needs more of.

So keep choosing to be better. Keep building yourself into more. Surround yourself with people who push you to grow. Keep asking questions. Keep seeking truth. And know this: the man you become won't just affect your own life. He'll shape the lives of others. The choices you make will echo. They'll reach your future family, your brothers, and even those who will come after you. That's legacy. And it begins with what you choose today.

This is the last day of this book, but it's not the end. From here on, it's your move.

⋄⋄⋄⋄⋄

💬 Reflection
Think about the type of person you're growing into. How do you show up every day? Are you stepping into the best version of yourself? As a knight in training, what does living with honour and purpose look like in your daily choices?

📓 Something to Write About
Write about a time when you faced a challenge and overcame it. What lessons did you learn? How did you stay true to your values in that moment? How can you apply those lessons to your journey as you move forward as a knight in training?

⚔ Challenge
Today, identify one action you can take that moves you closer to becoming the type of knight you want to be. It may be a small step, but it's one that keeps you on the path toward honour, integrity, and strength.

🧭 Code to Remember
I am a knight in training, and every day is a chance to grow stronger and ever more honourable. I will continue to build the life I want, one choice at a time.

CONCLUSION

If you've made it to this page, then you've already done something most don't—you showed up, stayed the course, and chose to think deeply about the kind of person you're becoming. That matters. For this, I applaud you. And this is just the beginning.

This book was never meant to give you all the answers. It was meant to give you something more important: the questions worth asking, the habits worth building, and the values worth living by. The path of a Knight in Training isn't a straight line—it's a lifelong commitment to growth, discipline, and honour. Some days will feel ridiculously easy. Other days will test everything you've got. But every day gives you a chance to choose who you're becoming.

With this book, you now have the tools to build something solid—something no one can take from you: your character, your word, your discipline, and your self-respect. Those things are forged, not given.

So, what's next? Well, that's up to you.

Keep reading. Keep learning. Keep showing up. Whether you realise it or not, you've already taken your first steps into manhood. And you're not walking alone.

The world is calling for good men. Not perfect—just real. Steady in storms, grounded in truth, brave in the face of fear. Be *that* man. And when others lose sight of who they are or who they could be, let your life remind them.

We'll meet again soon. Until then...

Hold the line. Walk with honour. And keep your sword sharp.

ACKNOWLEDGEMENTS

No man walks their path alone. Well, they shouldn't, anyway. I just wrote a whole book explaining why. But moving on...

This book—and the mission behind it—exists because of the people who've walked beside me, challenged me, believed in me, and stood with me through every step.

To my parents—thank you for the love, patience, and principles you planted early. Your guidance has shaped more than just this book—it shaped the guy who wrote it.

To the rest of my family (there are way too many of you, and you know who you are)—you are the most special group of idiots in the world, but you're *my* idiots, and I couldn't ask for better ones to be genetically tied to.

To my best mate Gabriel, my brother in all but blood—you've been there through the chaos and the peace. Your presence, loyalty, and laughter have kept me going more times than I can count.

To the ones who've tested my patience and challenged my character—you've shaped my resolve in ways I never asked for, but in the end, I'm grateful for the lessons. Whether you intended to or not, your actions played a role in the reason this book exists. Your negative influence has fuelled my desire to create a better path for those who need it, especially young men. Every destructive action has only made me more determined to build something positive.

In no particular order except alphabetical, here's to the real ones—friends, legends, and unexpected lifelines—who, knowingly or not, helped me through some rough patches. Some of you sent messages, some of you made me laugh when I needed it most, and some of you have no idea who I am. But still... thank you.

Amela T, Anastasia R, Andy S, Autumn S, Becca, Ben, Bex, Brianna F, Brittany B, Candice S, Charlie Riina, Carly M, Chris S, Cinthia, Citlalli, Colin Firth, Dan C, Daniela G, Deadpool, Deema K, Enrique R, Eric L, Eric V, Erin, Evan F, Frankie M, Freddy P, Gary Oldman, Henry, Huong V, Irma T, Jackie Chan, Jacob L, James, James K, Jason Statham, Johnnie, Johnny L, Jordan H, Joy C, Josh P, Joshua Z, Juan V, Justeena, Karina, Katie, Kendall J, Kyle R, Levi T, Martin, Milton V, Naomi K, Naomi S, Natalie J, Nick, Nicole C, Omar M, Pete G, Pierce Brosnan, Priscilla R, Quiana W, Quincy Villanueva, Rafa, Rebecca, Rico R, Rob, Robert Downey Jr, Robin M, Robyn, Ross E, Ryan P, Sam P, Samantha S, Sanjay S, Sean Connery, Sergio S, Shannon D, Sonia, Steffany C, Stephen Graham, Taran Egerton, Tashla C, Timothy Dalton, Toya R, Viviana G, Xavier A, and Zack P.

To Chicago, Empire of the Sun, FM-84, James Blunt, Let Em Riot, Lo-fi Girl, September 87, Supertramp, The Japanese House, The Kooks, The Midnight, and the many other artists on my Spotify playlists—thanks for keeping me awake with your musical awesomeness.

To everyone else I'd love to mention... I'd be typing for another bloody year to get you all in here. And honestly, I'm already tired, and pretty sure I have carpal tunnel now. So just know this—I think you're aces.

To the men of the growing MKC community—you are why these pages exist. This book is a torch we pass, heart to heart, building something lasting for those who will follow after us.

Thank you—all of you—for being part of this.
With strength, honour, and gratitude,

M

ABOUT THE AUTHOR

Michael Stonecastle is a mentor, writer, and founder of *The Modern Knights*—a movement devoted to restoring honour, discipline, and brotherhood among men of all ages, in a world that often forgets what true manhood means.

His work draws from timeless values, ancient wisdom, and hard-won lessons passed down through generations. Whether speaking to a young man just beginning his journey or to older men seeking to grow, guide, or rediscover themselves, Michael writes with one mission in mind: to help men live with strength, purpose, and integrity.

He believes every man deserves three things: a brotherhood to walk with, a code to live by, and a challenge worth rising to. Through this series, he speaks not as a perfect man, but as a fellow traveller—committed to walking the path of growth with those who are willing.

When he's not writing, he mentors across generations, leads workshops, and creates spaces where growth, discipline, and brotherhood are the standard.

If these pages resonated with you,
know that the journey doesn't end here.

For a compact companion built on the
same core principles, look for:

The Modern Knights Code:
The Pocket Book of Honour

Your compact standard.
Available wherever MKC titles are carried.

www.ingramcontent.com/pod-product-compliance
Lightning Source LLC
Chambersburg PA
CBHW040221040426
42333CB00049B/3029